GARRAWAY
FATHER
AND SON

GARRAWAY FATHER AND SON

ALLAN GARRAWAY

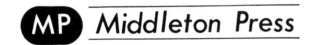

MP Middleton Press

Cover design –
Deborah Goodridge

First published 1985

ISBN 0 906520 20 7

© *1985 A.G.W. Garraway*

Phototypeset by CitySet Ltd, Chichester.

Published by Middleton Press
Easebourne Lane
Midhurst, West Sussex.
GU29 9AZ

Printed & bound by Biddles Ltd.,
Guildford and Kings Lynn.

CONTENTS

PREFACE

Several people tried to persuade Father to write down some of his memories of working on the railways, but he always said that he did not think that they would be of sufficient interest to either the general public or railway people. I have for long felt that this was not true and that his collection of photographs, particularly those of the Palestine Railways, should be more widely seen, because, like his 16mm cine films, much of it is almost unique. Middleton Press agreed to publish, and we hope that this mixture of his and my life stories will prove of interest. Apart from writing the Foreword, Dick Hardy has helped me considerably in writing about some of the trials and tribulations of my last years on the Festiniog Railway and I am, as always, extremely grateful to Dick for all his help.

I must thank Sue Roberts for transcribing my handwriting, and retyping much of it after I had edited it further, also thank John Slater, Editor of the Railway Magazine, for permission to use the map which originally appeared with some articles on the Palestine Railways in December 1936.

The photographs were nearly all taken by Father or myself except those on pages 15, 17 and 19 which were in my Father's office for as long as I can remember; those on pages 119 and 122 were by Geoff Charles, on page 136 was by G.L. Evans of Blaenau Ffestiniog, on page 145 by Norman Gurley, photographer to the FR, and on page 152 by Bill Roberton.

FOREWORD

The name of Garraway has been well known in railway circles for close on 60 years and this book, particularly at the beginning and towards its end shows us why.

Father Garraway is never likely to be forgotten by old time railwaymen in Cambridge. They remember him with pride for, as Assistant District Locomotive Superintendent, he ran the show under the light rein of his chief for many years. He knew railways and he knew men.

Young Allan, who shared with his Father a dedication not only to the profession but to the railway hobby, appeared on our footplate in sports jacket and flannels at Cambridge when we were running trials in 1946 with the newly rebuilt *Royal Sovereign*; since then our paths have crossed many times.

This book is a fascinating insight into the lives of Father and Son, so alike in many ways. The Father, who I met but once, I knew by reputation, indeed by legend, the Son virtually a contemporary. To read of an era prior to my own is always an education and reading about the life of a contemporary is especially fascinating, even if one knew a bit of what was going on. I have often wondered what Allan would have achieved had he stayed with British Railways but whilst nothing would really have induced me to leave what was to me the perfect life, he wanted a fresh challenge and so gave the rest of his working life to the service of the Festiniog Railway.

I did not become involved with this remarkable little railway and its staff and volunteers until 1977 when I was asked to join the Company Board. Certainly I had visited the railway, and worked on *Linda* with a conspicuous lack of success as a fireman but I had not realised how much things had changed from the original concept of the mid-fifties when trains rumbled across the Cob behind a petrol engined Simplex very well stricken in years. Allan, who like myself had had a vast practical experience of train working, could never have met the like of a Simplex passenger unit although I could claim to be one up for my very first footplate trip, which preceded a short journey on a South Eastern F1 *Flying Bedstead* by a few weeks, was on a Simplex tractor used in the construction of the Leatherhead bypass in 1933. Same thumping engine, same bag of bones gearbox and chains, same solemn progress.

Father and Son have shown great dedication to the cause in their well known and, by no means silent, way. Both men have created legends which are unlikely to die until railway lore becomes a thing of the past. Allan himself has played a leading part in the reincarnation of a remarkable little railway, and not many of us have gone away from our wedding reception by narrow gauge train. But then to transfer your newly wedded wife to the footplate of the rugged elbowing *Prince* driven by the charming speed merchant, William Hoole, demands a certain courage or zeal not given to us lesser mortals.

You will understand from what you read that the Festiniog Railway has a certain charisma, though hard pressed regular staff, including the General Manager, might not always think so. Although Allan would say that the Festiniog is different, main line and narrow gauge have everything in common, same problems, same heights, same depths, same indomitable will to rise to the occasion to achieve the impossible that marks the real railwayman. You will absorb all of this as the story of the lives of the two Garraways unfolds.

Dick Hardy. Chesham Bois, May 1985.

CHAPTER I

Ron –
early days and Palestine

Although the name Garraway is one of the less common surnames, it appears on a plaque in a wall in 'Change Alley' in the City of London, commemorating Garraways Coffee House, a famous hostelry where much important City business had been done in years gone by. There were Garraways at the siege of Londonderry of 1689 and for their services they were given a coat of arms. We can trace our ancestry back to this area, where there seem to have been several connected with the church in the 18th century. Harry Weldon Garraway, born 1857, married Katherine Robertson, hence our Scottish connection, and Ronald was their younger son, born in 1894 at Carshalton, Surrey, quite close to the *Windsor Castle* public house. From the house up to the Banstead Downs were farms and lavender fields, with cart roads on which Ron and his brother, Guy, used to play. Harry commuted to the City from Carshalton to London Bridge, which was then the main line of the London Brighton and South Coast Railway to Littlehampton, Bognor and Portsmouth.

The South Metropolitan Electric Tramway Coy had opened a route from West Croydon, through Waddon and Wallington to the *Windsor Castle* and Sutton, and Ron remembers the opening of a wooden plat-formed halt at Carshalton Beeches at which the push and pull operated local trains stopped. Railways interested Ron from an early age, but it was when he was unable to play games after having scarlet fever, that the interest grew. In those days, many of the South Coast Expresses divided (or amalgamated) at Sutton, one portion going to or from Victoria, and the other to or from London Bridge, which then was far more important than today. Where the Wimbledon line now drops away from the Epsom line, there were carriage sidings and the regular carriage pilot was no. 369 *Burgess Hill*, one of the 0–4–4 tanks, and her regular driver offered the schoolboy a ride to the carriage sidings. Another engine featuring in those memories was 61 *Ladysmith*, one of the B4 4–4–0s, whose regular turn was to work down to Sutton on a Victoria portion, before going back to London and then working a down express non-stop through Sutton later in the afternoon. Her driver was James Cook of Battersea, and he not only befriended the schoolboy on the platform but waved as he passed

1

through on the express. After James Cook had retired and father had become a railwayman, he managed to get his address from Battersea Shed and went to see him to tell him what it had all led to!

An 'O' gauge tinplate electric railway fostered this interest still more, but in those days there were very few materials for model railways, and most modelling was done on the larger gauges – 1, 2, etc. He started railway modelling in gauge 1, and naturally tried to model his favourite LB&SCR engines, which were the 13 4–4–2 tanks. In those days there were few drawings available from which to work, so he used to go to the station and mark off with chalk on the platform and pillars the positions of various items, and so build up his own drawings.

One of Ron's aunts was Mother Superior of a convent at Wantage. When Ron went to see her, and got out of the train at Wantage Road, he was surprised to find no engine on the front, for he had travelled in a slip coach, and so he decided that his railway must have such a vehicle! For the model the slip coupling was operated by a solenoid, which had come from an electric bell, energised from a special length of fourth rail which was placed in the track at some suitable point. The problem was speed and braking (or the lack of it), and it was quite an achievement to get it right so that the coach stopped in the station!

Ron's elder brother, Guy, had no interest in anything mechanical, but could do anything with horses, which became his life. Their very much younger sister, Ruth, was very close to Ron, and used to go with him to watch trains. When the family moved to Waddon, and had a house backing down to the railway she was able to tell the different classes of engine from the sound. As a girl she had croup and the doctor told her Mother that she was not to go out when the wind was in the east, and to help them know which way the wind was blowing Ron made them a weathervane, which of course had to be to the outline of one of his favourite 13s. My Auntie Ruth still recalls Ron cutting out the steel plate and the thrill of seeing the familiar outline appear.

When the time came for starting work, Ron wanted to go to Brighton Works, but railway jobs, particularly apprenticeships, were hard to come by unless you were the son of a railwayman, or could pull strings. Fortunately, Grandfather knew someone who had friends at Stratford, and so it came about that Ron went to Stratford Works of the GER as a premium apprentice, starting in January 1911. His service indenture makes interesting reading, particularly the wages paid! Like all such lads, he learnt his trade as a fitter and turner, but also went to night school to acquire academic qualifications, and was successful in winning a Director's Scholarship to East London College. Unfortunately, the First World War interrupted his studies, but nevertheless he passed the exams to become a member of the Institution of Civil Engineers which, as the senior institution, was the one most engineers of all callings preferred to join in those days. Amongst several special tasks he did whilst serving his apprenticeship was the job of making a valve gear model, which for many years was in the instruction train of the LNER which toured the loco depots, etc.

No. 25 and the slip coach on the gauge 1 railway about 1916.

When he completed his apprenticeship, he spent a period in the drawing office where he worked on the design and adaptation of machinery for making munitions before being sent to Temple Mills Wagon Works in charge of a gang of women on night shift on munitions work, a somewhat daunting task for a young man of 21. However, although the Railways were a reserved occupation, when the Army appealed for skilled people for the railway troops, father volunteered, was interviewed on 20th December 1917 by the GER, reported for brief military training at Bordon on 4th January 1918, was given three successive stripes in three days, and put on draft as a Sergeant by 24th January 1918.

He sailed from Southampton to Cherbourg, which they left in a troop train consisting of cattle wagons, at 2.45 pm on 9th February. Passing through Caen, Tours, and Bourges, they stopped for several hours at St. Caiez on the 10th, owing to a breakdown. They reached St. Germain at 3.15 pm on the 11th, and went to a rest camp and departed from there at 12.44 am on the 12th, travelling down the Rhone Valley to Avignon 2.30 pm, and Marseilles 11.30 pm. Continuing through Toulon 8.30 am on the 13th and along the Mediterranean Coast, they reached Ventimiglia at 2.00 am on the 14th. The Italians were very enthusiastic about the British and showered the train with apples and oranges at stations. The train was split into two to cross the Apennine Mountains, with two electric locos for each portion of the train, and they reached Modena at 8.00 am on the 15th, and Faenza at midday, where they spent the afternoon at a further rest camp. Leaving at 7.00 pm, they passed Ancona next morning and

3

reached Foggia at 2.30 am on the 17th where they remained until 8.00 am, waking up wet through, with it very cold, raining and snow. They reached Brindisi at 9.30 pm, and Taranto at 6.30 am on the 18th. Not exactly high speed travel, and all in a cattle truck in the winter!

They crossed to Alexandria in the "Kashgar" with a Japanese and Italian escort and on 1st March, Ron finally arrived at Kantara, to find that he was not really needed there. At the end of the month he was sent up to Ludd (Lydda) as a loco examiner, but after a while he was back at Kantara and became Foreman Fitter in the Running Shed as Quartermaster Sergeant, and finally Chief Works Foreman with charge of the breakdown train, as a 2nd Class Warrant Officer, the highest rank then obtainable.

With the end of the War, he got his camera sent out, which took postcard size photographs on roll film. Although, unfortunately, the quality of many of the photographs is not very good, chiefly due to slow shutter speeds and camera faults, with such a large size negative a small amount of enlarging produces a large photograph, which with modern papers can be very good. He also got prints from one or two friends' negatives.

The Turks (Ottoman Empire) had built 105 cms (3'6") gauge lines south from Turkey through Syria to Damascus, Beyrut (Beirut) and **Haifa into Palestine**, and down towards Egypt. As our Forces, under **Allenby**, pushed the Turks back, they rebuilt the railway to standard **gauge as far as Haifa**, and eventually also rebuilt the metre gauge Ludd

Kantara Works. The erecting shop in November 1919.

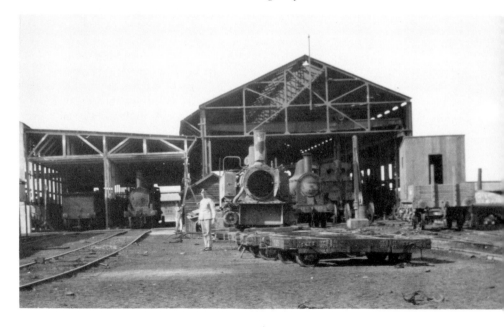

4

An ex-LSWR 0–6–0 on the Palestine Military Railway.

(Lydda) – Jerusalem line to standard gauge. There was a 60 cm gauge line to Jaffa and also from Jerusalem to Ram Allah, for which there were Baldwin and Hunslet 4–6–0 tanks. For working the standard gauge there were Egyptian State Railway engines, as well as ex-LNWR Cauliflowers, which ended up as buffer stops at Kantara, and were then scrapped! There were also LSWR 0–6–0s which worked the more important ambulance and passenger trains together with some Baldwin 2–6–0s very similar to those imported onto the Midland and GN railways at the turn of the century in Britain, as well as Manning Wardle 0–6–0 tanks, captured German engines, etc. After the War, some American Baldwin 'H' class 4–6–0s were delivered in pieces and these were assembled at Kantara.

From Haifa the 105 cm line ran inland to Deraa which was the junction for Maan and the Hedjaz Railway to Medina which Lawrence had blown up. This line continued to Damascus and thence north to Homs and Aleppo and into Turkey, but a branch continued over the Lebanon Mountains, with rack locomotives to Beyrut (Beirut).

At the beginning of September 1919, Ron and his friend Jack McCallum had some leave and went for a trip to Haifa and then over the 3'6" gauge line to Damascus and Beyrut. On the return they visited Jerusalem and the holy places. His description of the journey fills 20 pages of foolscap and there are other sheets describing in detail the photographs which he sent both to his home and also to his fiancee. Many of the rail-

5

A rack engine in the Lebanon Mountains on the Damascus-Beirut line.

way lines are no more, and the descriptions and photographs are of rare interest today. As they were both involved with the Railways, they were able to arrange with the RTO to travel on the 'posh' train which was the only through train from Kantara to Haifa and was normally reserved for officers only. Ron and Jack left Kantara on this train at about 11.00 pm on Sunday night, and got to Ludd at about 7.00 am in the morning, where they went to the mess and had breakfast, getting some hot water from the engine for a mess tin wash and shave! Leaving Ludd at about 8.30 am, they arrived at Haifa for lunch and had an exciting trip in a Ford taxi to the top of Mount Carmel.

The next morning, they left Haifa at 11.00 am, with a train of seven bogie corridor coaches on the 3'6" gauge which went inland to Afule and the descent to the Jordan Valley and the Sea of Galilee. After crossing the Jordan on a high steel girder bridge and recrossing it on a timber trestle replacing one blown up in the War, which is the lowest point of the journey, the line climbs on a ledge on the hillside with severe curves and horseshoe bends, going up one side of a valley and back the other side. At one point they passed the remains of a tender lying about 500 feet below; it had broken away from an engine going up the hill! Eventually the line reaches a plateau in the Lebanon mountains, the land of the King of Hedjaz. The junction of Deraa was reached at about 5.30 pm. There the train reversed and, after seeing a beautiful sunset over snowcapped

Mount Lebanon, Damascus was reached at about 10.30pm. As they approached the station the train was shot at by Bedouins, who went around armed to the teeth – a peculiar practice which had been causing anxiety for some time! They stayed in a rest camp at the end of the station, but found it a bit cold and had to sleep together to conserve blankets and warmth. Next morning they washed in a stream, had breakfast in the town, and left at 7.45am for another scenic run, though the line was not perched quite so precariously on the mountainside. Plenty of clear water was gushing out of the rocks, and orchards everywhere, with every class of fruit, were the main features of the scenery. After climbing to start with, the line dropped into the Bekaa Valley, and then at Molakka the engine was changed for the rack section. Speed was only walking pace, with three stops for water before reaching the summit, at about 9,000 feet above sea level, a station with only a train length of level track before the start of the descent to Beyrut with the line again on ledges on the hillside with precipitous drops below. There were two reversing stations on this run. Beyrut then was torn with dissent as some of the populace wanted British rule, some French, some American. The British were not allowed out at night unless armed and in parties. Ron and Jack spent a day there taking a

A view from the Railway Operating Division billet at Haifa, with the narrow gauge lines in foreground.

7

In the Yarmak Valley

tram to the pine forests and exploring the town and harbour, where a Turkish cruiser had been scuttled in the fairway. They had hoped to return to Haifa by sea, but the ship was not running, so they did the same two day rail trip where the passengers were travelling on every buffer, side steps, or anywhere they could hang on to!

The foreign custom of men first, women and children to follow, upset Ron, so they made out that their compartment was reserved for troops, but just before departure they invited two families with a baby and a little girl to join them who were very grateful and "it was quite pathetic to see their relief".

After reaching the summit, the descent was made at a good speed, which made them a trifle apprehensive, with the railway being on a ledge with 400'-500' drops on one side and continuous sharp curves. They had difficulty in finding a hotel in Damascus as they were all out of bounds to "other ranks", to their disgust, but eventually an English lady directed them to the only hotel in bounds.

Next day their train to Haifa had a special saloon at the back for a Hedjaz Prince, and the attentions paid to him by everyone caused Ron some amusement.

On return to Kantara, life was never dull, as extracts from a letter dated 15th October 1919 shows. "A fortnight ago, one of our trains broke away from the engine, and the driver very foolishly waited for it, with the

8

Beirut Harbour with a sunken Turkish cruiser

result that when it caught him up, the front coach showed its affection by snuggling up with the tender, and the next two coaches telescoped! Last week, whilst shunting in the goods yard, some wagons refused to follow the path that's straight, and of course we had to run out and by means of our crane, etc., lift them back to the rails again. On Monday morning about 5 am, when I was enjoying the good old sleep, someone set the points wrongly and one of the engines, instead of going along the right road, was turned into a dead end at the end of which there were no stops! He went gaily sailing along at full steam until the rails stopped, and then over the top and across the desert!! When I found him he was up to his axles in sand with a tendency to lie on his side, and the tender running first had made quite a sand bank and half buried itself! That's Monday. Tuesday morning, whilst in the shops, I received a telephone message saying that the breakdown crane had capsized, and I nearly did the same! I got my gang together – all natives who can't speak a word of English, and have about as much idea of doing a job as our old Tom Cat! When I found it, I realised what lay before us. The breakdown crane – a huge 30 ton capacity steam travelling crane weighing about 50-60 tons, had attempted to unload some stores material, and, being too heavy, had crashed over on its side! I have got a 20 ton steam crane to do the job but must naturally dismantle a good deal first. Yesterday we got the boiler and tanks off, this morning the jib. This morning we have begun to turn her over again, but, my word, it's a big job, and when all your men are natives bar the crane driver, it caused some anxious moments at times. I think if we have a bit of luck we should be finished tomorrow, and then I shall have the old dear to repair in the Erecting Shop. Oh! it's a lovely war, or is it peace? Administrative units work just the same in either, and now that civilian labour has

9

George Richard Smith and the steam launch on the Broads.

Toftwood Mill, E. Dereham.

almost replaced the troops and acts only under military supervision, the troubles begin. I never saw in all my life such a useless, worthless race of people as the Egyptians. They know nothing, can do nothing, and yet parade the streets crying 'Egypt for the Egyptians!' They couldn't govern a cat's meat business, let alone run one!"

At the end of January 1920, he reported to Demob Camp and left Alexandria on *SS Kursk* on 20th February. They visited Malta, and as the Captain was anxious to give everyone an enjoyable voyage they followed the African Coast as much as possible. After calling at Gibraltar they kept land in sight all day, but had to reduce speed in the Channel, owing to fog, and anchored in Plymouth Sound on 29th February at 10.30 am. Next day they travelled by the LSWR to Waterloo. Their journey home had been much quicker than that going out!

CHAPTER II

Cambridge and Lincoln

Ron straightaway returned to Stratford and almost at once was appointed to take charge of the GER locomotives which were being overhauled at Woolwich Arsenal. Upon completion of this work, he was sent to Doncaster with the special duties of investigating the hot boxes on wagons on the GN and GE joint line from there through Lincoln to Spalding and March. In September 1921 he was sent to Peterborough East as Assistant Depot Superintendent, marrying in January 1922, and being appointed Depot Superintendent in March.

His wife, Connie Smith, was a farmer's daughter from Toftwood, Dereham. Her father had wanted to be an engineer, but was made to go into farming. He had one of the first cars in the neighbourhood, much of his farm machinery was driven by steam, and he also had a steam launch on the Broads. He retained the windmill, purely for love of machinery, and I still have tools stamped with *G.R. Smith*. The Smith family are connected with the Vasseurs, who founded Poughkeepsie College, New York State; George's wife was a Bishop, of the family which founded the furniture removers and depositories, whose name can be seen on leaving Victoria Station, London.

After the grouping, the GE shed at Peterborough was put under the administration of the GN at New England, and the development of March and its yard took away much of its importance.

In 1924 Ron moved to Cambridge as Assistant District Loco Superintendent. Whilst at Cambridge, he saw the development of the marshalling yard at Whitemoor (March) which became the largest depot in the district. The Up Yard had the Frolich hydraulic retarders, identical to those in Hamm Yard, Germany, whereas the Down Yard had electro magnetic retarders. To supply electricity for the Yard, the LNER built its own power station, as the Power Company had wanted to charge an exhorbitant amount to bring sufficient electric power to the area; there was no grid system in those days.

Cambridge Depot itself was modernised and rebuilt in the '30s with a coaling plant, wheel drop, hot water washing out plant, etc., and had an allocation of over 100 engines. These ranged from B17s and B12s for the Liverpool Street services, GN Atlantics for the King's Cross Buffet Services, with *Claud Hamiltons* in their various forms for the less important workings. The local cross country services to Mildenhall and Haverhill

GE no. 203 after a rebuild at Woolwich Arsenal in 1920.

were entrusted to E4 "Intermediate" 2–4–0s as well as J15s. Freight services were mostly worked by the various GE 0–6–0s; the heavy O2 and O4 2–8–0s were at Whitemoor for the Temple Mills Coal Trains. There were 2–4–2s of F3, etc., for carriage shunting as well as "Buck Jumpers" (J67, J68 and J69) for shunting. The LMS also stabled one or two engines for the Bletchley and Kettering trains.

Father's particular pride and joy were the two Royal Clauds, 8783 and 8787, the former with the last GER copper capped chimney. There was a special link for the three Royal train drivers who worked to King's Cross and King's Lynn every day, the two engines doing likewise, and he would not let the Royal engines be handled by anyone else. To see those engines shining when ready for a Royal working was a beautiful sight.

Unfortunately, 8783 hit a lorry of hay at Hilgay in 1939 and was badly damaged, so that she was rebuilt with the larger boiler, and, though green, was not the same. Several people were killed in the accident as the side of the train was ripped out by wagons standing in the siding. Father was there all night cleaning up the wreckage and was annoyed next day to see his Royal driver driving the same working; someone had forgotten to alter the roster, but the driver said it was best to be out on the job or he might have lost his nerve.

Father at his desk at Cambridge, 1936.

South Lynn, M & GN.

In those days the Royal Train was used quite frequently, sometimes at quite short notice. King George V spent long periods at Sandringham and then slipped up to London for two or three days. He died at Sandringham, and the Royal Engines had already been prepared, but then the train was made heavier and it was decided to use a B17. Unfortunately, no. 2800 *Sandringham* was in pieces in Stratford Works, and the LNER would not resort to name swapping, so the best B17 available was brought in off her booked working, washed out, cleaned and coaled overnight. Father had an anxious time as she had a joint blowing slightly which they preferred not to disturb, but she did the job without any hitch.

The Special Notices for this Royal Working include the note that the timings must be kept private, yet there were goodly crowds everywhere to see the train.

The old GER had organised the loco Running Department into very small Districts. Even under the LNER, and to some extent even today, the GER lines remain a very independent organisation, as they have relatively little interconnection with the rest of the country.

The caption as written up by Father in later years.

Peterborough East Circa 1923.

Time Clerk Clerk Running Foreman Run. Foreman. Staff Clerk. C.&W. Foreⁿ Chief Clerk Junior
Brown Chapman Dunn Running Taylor
Wagon Foreman Boiler Foreman Shed Master. Foreman fitter Running Foreman
Collinesk. Blundell. R.H.R. Garraway Fletcher. Ted Balls.

15

This notice is, and must be kept, strictly private.

LONDON & NORTH EASTERN RAILWAY

S.739.36

Special Train
Notice No. R 60.

Liverpool Street Station,

22nd January, 1936.

NOTICE OF

A Special Passenger Train

CONVEYING

MEMBERS OF THE ROYAL FAMILY

AND THE REMAINS OF HIS MAJESTY

KING GEORGE V.,

FROM

WOLFERTON TO KING'S CROSS

ON

Thursday, 23rd January, 1936.

The undermentioned to **wire promptly** *"Superintendent, 61," Liverpool Street, acknowledging receipt of this Notice in the following code "R. 60."*

King's Cross to Hitchin inclusive.	*Shelford.*	*Ely to King's Lynn inclusive.*
Letchworth to Harston inclusive.	*Cambridge.*	*Goods Agent, King's Lynn.*
Stroud Green.	*D.S. Cambridge.*	*North Wootton to Hunstanton inclusive.*
Crouch End.	*Goods Agent, Cambridge.*	
Highgate.	*Barnwell Junction.*	
	Waterbeach.	

During the 30s Ipswich was given up as a District, leaving only the Stratford, Cambridge and Norwich Districts. Stratford was the biggest District; in fact Stratford was the biggest loco depot in the world, and took over Bishops Stortford from Cambridge, but they in turn took over Bury St. Edmunds. Then, when the Midland & Great Northern Joint Railway operating and loco department was wholly taken over by the LNER in 1937, South Lynn, the largest M&GN shed, was added and Mr. Turbott, the Shed Master, became another of my kind friends.

The M&GN worked fantastic loads with little engines over a single track railway whose gradient profile strongly resembled the teeth of a saw. In the summer months the excursion and Saturday traffic from the Midlands to Yarmouth, Cromer, etc., was extremely heavy, yet trains were worked by very competent enginemen with little 4–4–0s. The line had the Whitaker tablet exchange apparatus so that trains did not have to slow up to exchange tokens; it was a fascinating sight to see a train pass through at speed, and to see the virtually instantaneous action of one token go onto the engine and the one from the engine be left swinging on

Cambridge staff.

17

the hook. It was only by this means that the engines could get a good run down the banks and up the next one; without it they could never have got the traffic through.

After the grouping the Southern Area Loco Running Department of the LNER came under WGP Maclure, who was an old Great Gentral Railway man. He, naturally, tended to promote people he knew from the GCR, and he was followed in 1931 by ISW Groom, who was an ex-GNR man. His promotions were, in some cases, a little odd and Ron, as a GER man, did not get a look in. With the War, the Southern Area was split into two, and the three Great Eastern districts became the Eastern Section, whilst the GN and GC districts became the Western Section. In 1941 Ron was appointed District Loco Superintendent at Lincoln, in the Western Section, the headquarters of which, for the War, was at Gerrards Cross.

The Lincoln District was a medium-sized one, and to attempt to even out the size of districts, Langwith, near Shirebrook, was transferred from the Colwick, Nottingham District to Lincoln. Langwith, with about 60 engines, was essentially a freight depot, on the old Lancashire, Derby-

Constructing Cambridge coaling plant, 7th December 1931.

18

Presentation to W.G.P. Maclure, Loco Running Sup.ᵗ 20-3-1931 at G.N. Hotel Peterboro'

District Loco Superintendents and their assistants, 20th March 1931.

shire and East Coast Railway, a line which never reached its goals, only extending from Chesterfield to Pyewipe Junction, just north of Lincoln. Apart from a local passenger service, it served a considerable number of collieries, with heavy coal traffic mostly to Lincoln for the joint line to Whitemoor but a certain amount going on to the GN main line at Tuxford, where the railway workshops had been situated, and which had another small shed. At Langwith there were connections north towards Sheffield up the Clowne branch and southwards to Mansfield. The LD and ECR had its own engines, and some, LNER Class M1, still survived and were based at Tuxford, which had about 15 engines. Lincoln, pregrouping, had had three sheds, the GER at Pyewipe, the GCR by Durham Ox Crossing – now the site of the Diesel Depot – and the GN by Brayford Water. The GN shed had become the Lincoln depot, which had about sixty engines, but like other depots of mixed ancestry, retained many peculiar anachronisms, with staff working under different conditions according to whether they were ex-GC or otherwise.

Immingham with Grimsby was the biggest depot with 120 engines. Grimsby had depots for both the GN and GC, but when Sir Sam Fay had

19

The new engine shed under construction at Whitemoor, March on 26th April 1932.

constructed Immingham docks, a new depot had been built there, and Grimsby was only used for servicing and as a signing on point for men. Boston, a small rural shed with 40 engines gained some importance in the '50s with its men working the London trains, as I shall recount later. The small shed at Louth, with nine engines, completed the District.

The engines from Lincoln District depots rarely featured in exciting performances, in fact it was an area little heard about in general. Most of its passenger workings were rural local passenger services, the only trains of note being the predecessor of the North Country Continental, revived soon after the War – initially, primarily for troops! This came up the Joint Line and at various times went to Manchester and/or York, sometimes as separate trains. Initially it was mostly B17 worked, with the GC 4–6–0s occasionally participating, but as B1s became more numerous they were more commonly used. From Cleethorpes and Grimsby there was a through train to London, and others to Manchester, and soon after nationalisation a through train via Lincoln to Nottingham and Birmingham was introduced. Immingham had the GC compound Atlantics, which mostly worked to Sheffield; so long as they remained with Immingham men, who were used to them, they did good if mundane work, but if they perchance fell into the hands of strangers, problems tended to arise. Of the freight workings there were the fully fitted fish trains from Grimsby to London and Banbury for the GWR and elsewhere, which were as important as passenger workings as far as performance and time-

No. 8783, the Royal Engine, and other exhibits at the Railway Exhibition, Cambridge, 1937.

keeping were concerned. Sugar beet traffic, as well as potatoes and other agricultural produce, occurred in the appropriate seasons. The Joint Line was dominated by coal traffic, from the Derbyshire coalfield via the LD&ECR line through Tuxford, and the Yorkshire coalfield via Doncaster, en route to Whitemoor (March) for London and East Anglia.

Lincoln was a town bedevilled by three level crossings, the High Street at the north end of the station and the Durham Ox at the south end. There was also one at the south end of the Midland station, which, fortunately, was far less used. There was an avoiding line from Pyewipe Junction to Greetwell and Washingborough Junctions which enabled Joint Line or Boston line trains to avoid the town, but anything from Honington and Grantham or New Holland and Grimsby had to go through the station, and this included the very heavy High Dyke (Grantham) to Frodingham iron ore trains, which had to rumble through the station to Pyewipe to be re-engined and reverse back through the station again. Being unfitted, these trains, particularly loaded, were slowmoving, and their length was such that they had to approach very slowly and if checked at the second crossing, blocked the first one. The Durham Ox crossing was right on top of the rail crossing between the connection from the LMS to the New Holland line and the main line from the station.

21

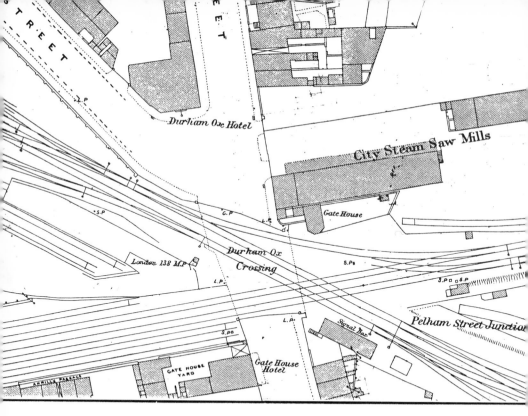

The Durham Ox Crossing, Lincoln.

After the War, the summer passenger traffic to the resorts of Clee-thorpes, Skegness and, to a lesser extent, Sutton and Mablethorpe, necessitated very many extra workings, timetabled as well as duplicated, and day excursions. Most of the Cleethorpes traffic came from Sheffield and Doncaster, but there was some coming in through Lincoln from the Midlands as well as from London, similarly, to Skegness, Sutton and Mablethorpe. On Sundays and August Bank Holiday which, in those days was at the beginning of the month, there was a continual stream of trains coming in which had to be stabled, the engines turned and serviced before return at night, and the inspectors were on duty at key points to assist. Ron and the Shed Masters were also very much around watching what was happening, and usually there would be some poor old crock pressed into passenger service who would limp into its destination late, and need replacement for the return working. On the Sutton and Mable-thorpe loop there was no ordinary Sunday service, so the north end of the branch was closed, and the trains were stabled nose to tail towards Louth. This necessitated the last arrival being first to return. If the weather was fine, many of the crews joined in the seaside activities, but if the weather was poor, there were problems as the only place for them to go was the small Porter's Room. There was a need for a small messroom, but the Railway Executive had laid down minimum standards for messroom accommodation, requiring so many washbasins, toilets, etc., depending upon average and maximum user. To meet these requirements required a

22

palatial edifice, for use on about a dozen weekends a year; the rest of the time it would have been locked up. It so happened that at the time I was in the section at headquarters dealing with such matters, and my Father asked me if some commonsense couldn't be brought to bear so that a small prefabricated structure at moderate cost could be provided to give crews somewhere for them to go. I did manage to get agreement that it should be considered as a special case, but I don't think anything ever happened. Not only the branch, but the main East Lincolnshire line from Grimsby to Spalding has been closed, with only odd bits remaining for freight.

Ron was asked to move from Lincoln to larger Districts, but he said that he had achieved his ambition of running a District. With wartime and post war housing problems, he asked that he might be allowed to remain at Lincoln, so he was able to run the District until he retired at the end of December 1954. Consequently, he built up a team of people who knew him and what he wanted, and the Lincoln District had a reputation for being one of the happiest on the Eastern Region. With the onset of diesel-isation – the Lincolnshire railcar scheme was the second on British Rail – he realised that there was going to be a lot of reorganisation, and work for which he would never see the benefit, so he decided to retire so that he could enjoy life whilst still young enough to do so.

He and his wife moved back to Surrey where they had a house at Cheam backing down to the same line near which he had been born, though its Portsmouth trains had become EMUs and steam only appeared on the occasional freights. He then became involved with the Festiniog Railway as a Director of the Society, and was for years its financial and membership secretary. Apart from the very considerable amount of work this entailed – and he was an engineer, not an accountant – he spent a lot of time at Porthmadog giving assistance mostly at Boston Lodge. There was one occasion when I had to press him into assisting on the train, and when I checked the ticket sales that night was surprised at the number of dog tickets. It transpired he had sold them instead of Observation Car tickets, for the supplementary fare.

Connie was not going to sit around doing nothing, and worked very hard on the Buffet Cars, serving refreshments and drinks etc. They also came up on several occasions solely to give help on special trains, particularly where a meal was being served, and for the Society A.G.M. special trains Auntie Ruth was usually with them, and she also helped.

As the membership grew, so the task became more than he could manage, and it had to be divided into various sections. Illness finally forced him to give up specific duties, but he was appointed a Society Vice President, and he attended meetings whenever possible, his advice as an elder statesman being much appreciated. The last time I saw him was at a joint Company and Society meeting at the Great Northern Hotel, Kings Cross, when he said to me that he felt that it was becoming rather too much for him to travel up to London. He passed away peacefuly in his sleep in the early hours of 9th August 1972, having been working on a model in his workshop the evening before.

23

CHAPTER III

Allan –
early days and Germany

I was born in 1926, and as a child showed a great interest in railways and steam engines. I can remember in my earliest days wanting to go to the 'Gapes', which was what I called the level crossing by Trumpington Signal Box, on Long Road, Cambridge. I wasn't much older before the signal box had to be moved a few yards to enable the bridge to be built to replace the level crossing, and whilst this was in progress a temporary level crossing was put in at the other side of the signal box. At an early age I was given clockwork Hornby railway equipment, which I steadily developed. Father retrieved the Gauge 1 railway from the shed roof of the family home, and built it up into a small layout which just fitted into the living room. Unfortunately, in doing this it had minimum radius curves, of three foot radius, which are sharp for Gauge 0, but terrible on Gauge 1. The motor of no. 25, the 13 tank, was very poor and Father and I went to Bassett Lowke's Northampton Works to see about getting a new one, but their new motors were a trifle larger and would not fit. Their staff were most interested, though, to see such a motor, then about twenty years old. The only solution was to build a new engine, and so no. 26 came into being, a somewhat better model too.

The layout developed a little, but its most interesting feature was the signalling on one section. The layout was unprototypical, and signalling was in no way complete, but it was designed for both ways running. The 17 lever frame was fully interlocked, and the signal levers had proper catches, though with no springs, and Father was told that it would never work, and if it did, would soon break. It has had many years of use by careful fingers, and is still working with not one failure! Although the Bassett Lowke motors were only 8 volt, the railway was operated on 12 volt, by means of a long cable from the garage plugged into the car. It was only during the War when I modified the layout and used it in the garden during the summer holidays that we used an accumulator charged at night!

At the time I was born, Mother and Father were very friendly with the Cambridge LMS Goods Agent, who had a son, Peter, who was a little older than I. They moved to Hagley, the next station to Stourbridge Junction on the line to Kidderminster and with a neighbour, Rob Davies,

24

The gauge 1 railway in the garden at Cambridge, 1940.

developed an 'O' gauge layout round their attic. In school holidays, Peter and I used to stay with each other and go 'spotting' at Stafford, Birmingham Snow Hill, Hitchin, etc., and we also took a few photographs. Rob Davies went to Crewe Loco Works and then went with the Crown Agents, first to Palestine and then Kenya. They gave up their 'O' gauge when they left home in the War, and I acquired what I could afford, and developed my own gauge 'O' layout to coarse scale standards. The Gauge 1 languished in the garage, as it was a major undertaking to assemble the layout and necessitated the assurance of a fine day. One day, Peter asked us if he might restore it again as he had rooms large enough for it, and finally he has bought it so that he can develop it as he wants. Perhaps if Father had built it differently, and I had not acquired Peter's 'O' gauge material – and if I could have seen how my life would change – I would have developed the '1' gauge; some modern motors would have been fitted to the engines, particularly old 25, and would have hauled much more realistic loads than the old Bassett Lowke 8 volt motors, even on 12 volts.

Apart from model railways at home, I took every opportunity of accompanying Father on his trips round the Cambridge District, as well as visiting Cambridge Shed whenever possible. Walter Billing, the Mechanical Foreman, was a particular friend of mine, and as an 11 or 12 year old schoolboy I went to the shed with Father on Saturday mornings and usually spent the time with Mr. Billing who took me around with him. If an A4 had come down from King's Cross on a running in turn he would

The author when 6 years old and the then new coaling plant at Cambridge.

put me on the engine when it went off shed and I would ride through Cambridge Station and then back onto the King's Cross train in the bay platform. Sometimes, perhaps because he wanted to get rid of me to get on with his own work, he would put me on the GE 0–6–0 tank which was shunting the shed. Sometimes, I was even allowed to work the regulator and brake, and I can recall both shunting the shed and backing A4s onto trains.

If there was a breakdown in holidaytime, Father would telephone home and I would cycle as fast as I could to the Shed to catch the breakdown train, and in this way gained some useful insight into breakdown work.

When I was ten years old I became interested in cameras. Father was wanting to get a cine camera and I recall that we tried out equipment at 8mm, 9.5mm and 16mm at home, but in those days there was no compari-

Derailment at South Lynn, 8th April 1940.

son, so we had 16mm. The little cine Kodak camera was relatively cheap, but its lens was surprisingly good, and I am still using it today. With clockwork drive, it is very old fashioned – and so is 16mm for amateurs, but having all the equipment, why start afresh at this time of life? Nevertheless, when we had it, Father said that we didn't really want any more cameras in the family, and I could use the little vest pocket Kodak, which took size 127 films. He would buy me films for a year, and I straight away went down Long Road to take my first photographs.

Unfortunately, Father took very few railway photos after he came back from Palestine and Egypt, but I made up for it in a boyish way, recording not only the everyday engines, but scenes wherever I went. It was only when I went to Germany and could acquire better cameras very cheaply that the vest pocket Kodak was put to one side, but it continued for certain uses.

I first went to school in Cambridge but, with the uncertainties of railway life, Father was anxious that I should be at boarding school, so I went to The Leys. In 1940 their premises were suddenly requisitioned and they

One of my first photographs; an 02 on an up 'target' train leaving the reception siding at Trumpington.

moved to the Atholl Palace Hotel at Pitlochry, and for four years I used every opportunity to explore the area as much as I could by bicycle. It also necessitated long wartime rail journeys, including one through York the day after one of its big air raids, when only one platform was in use and trains were shunted out again and sent round the avoiding line. Apart from introducing me to the beauties of Scotland, it also gave me a chance to see engines working hard up the long climb through Pitlochry, with double headed black fives on most trains, and the smaller ex-Caledonian Railway engines working the Perth-Struan locals. On occasions there was an ex-Highland Railway "Castle" to be seen, and once, when walking up to the town, I was startled by the sound of a shrill whistle, an unfamiliar sound for the Highlands, and a Midland Compound came up the gradient on a local. I have since read of this unusual event, caused presumably by an engine failure.

I went back to Cambridge to go to the University, reading Engineering at St Catharine's College, with Arthur Cook, the author and expert on LNER locomotives, as my Director of Studies. He persuaded me to join the Stephenson Locomotive Society, and I was also a member of the University Railway Club, but I did not do much of a railway nature, as I felt that that could wait. I did on occasion visit the shed and meet Father's successor, TCB Miller, with whom I was to work later, and he very kindly contrived for me to ride to Bishops Stortford on no. 1671 *Royal Sovereign*, one of the B17s rebuilt with two cylinders, and kept as the Royal engine. Dick Hardy was riding with the engine as well, as he recounts in the Foreword to this book.

I had never been any good at ball games at school, but had always wanted to row, so I joined the Rowing Club, and, in spite of being only around 10 stone in weight, got into the 2nd VIII. In the Lent bump races in 1945 we made a bump on each night, which entitled us to our oars, but with shortages we had to wait until an oar got broken before we could actually have one. It was an extraordinary crew, only one man had done any rowing previously. We were all very light (bow was only 9 stone) and yet in practice, just before the races, the 1st VIII had had difficulty in catching us to practise making a bump! Three of the crew were on cadet courses and so left at the end of that term, and the summer term crew never went quite as well, but it was again unusual, for a second division crew, in being bumped on its first night, making an overbump second night (i.e. bumping the crew three in front, the two crews immediately in front having already bumped) and then being bumped yet again by the same crew.

I experienced great difficulty with the mathematics involved in much of the work, and did not do sufficiently well in the 2nd year May exams to continue to get deferment from call-up. I was able to take the autumn examinations, which qualified me for a degree, but in the meantime I had been to a War Office Selection Board at Fernhurst in West Sussex, and had been accepted for training for a commission in the Royal Engineers. After the obligatory primary training at Pontefract (on the way meeting someone with whom I had done a practical at Cambridge, which helped those first hours in the army) I went to basic R.E. training at Farnborough, where I was with one or two others ex-Cambridge, as well as several from other universities, including John Dalison, who later became very active with the Festiniog East Anglian Group.

When on Officer Cadet training at Newark, I applied for, and was accepted for, training in Railway Operating, and went to Longmoor, where I duly became 2nd Lieutenant. The 16-week course was in two parts. The first eight weeks were spent on railway operating, and the second eight weeks on locomotive work, and involved a certain amount of practical work as well as time in classrooms. The Longmoor Military Railway at that time was mostly worked by W.D. 0–6–0 tanks, but there were also two W.D. 2–8–0s, as well as one of the American 2–8–0s, and an American 0–6–0 tank. Some of the Dean 0–6–0s, as well as the varied assortment of engines which had worked on the line, including two I2 tanks, were stored in the sidings towards Liphook. We also spent two or three days re-railing the old M & GN 4–4–0 *Kingsley* which another training class had previously thrown off. The footplate work on the Longmoor Military Railway was not very exacting, and really only gave an insight into what it was like, so I asked Father whether there was any possibility of getting out with his Chief Inspector, George Emerson. To regularise matters, Father spoke to his chief, George Musgrave, himself an old Sapper, who readily agreed and issued a footplate pass for me. I was due for my commissioning leave at the end of the course and I spent most of it with George Emmerson, who showed me the basics of how and when to fire, and how to handle the engine, on stopping trains mostly between Grimsby and Gainsborough, whilst he in turn either checked on engines or was passing out firemen as fit to drive, i.e. to become Passed Firemen.

This limited experience was to prove invaluable to me, as I was posted to Germany where the 348 Railway Operating Squadron (ex 153 of wartime days) was operating the normal services on a branch of the Reichsbahn as a Training Operation. This branch was a single line, from Herford, on the main East to West trunk route from Hamm and Bielefeld to Hannover, running south through Detmold, where we were based, to Himmighausen where it joined the Hameln – Paderborn line. North of Detmold at Lage the line crossed another branch running from Bielefeld to Hameln, though that line didn't run into Hameln as the bridge over the Weser had been demolished in the War.

The Detmold Military Railway was operated on British Military signalling regulations, but using the German signals, i.e. it used miniature electric staff. The Germans, however, had two signal boxes at each crossing loop, one at each end, so the line was operated as a double line through the stations. At the junctions, Herford, Lage and Hemighausen, we had Military signalmen working with the Germans. Several of the stations and loops were switched out so that they became staffed halts. The engine allocation was three of the ubiquitous 38 class 4–6–0s, five of the 50 class 2–10–0s, and two of the 92 class 0–8–0 tanks, also a 350 hp English Electric diesel shunter and a German 360 hp shunter with Voith

Detmold station and shed. The tall chimney helped take smoke from engines high into the atmosphere, as well as helping the fire when first lit up.

hydraulic transmission. There was also a four-wheeled German Railbus. We had three passenger diagrams, two worked all day, one in the afternoon only, two freight workings double shifted, and two shunt workings, one of which was supposed to be a diesel, at Bad Salzufflen.

When I got to Detmold in December 1947 I was told that I was going to take over as Loco Superintendent. Within a few days of arriving I was called out in the evening to a breakdown which typified the slap-happy way much of the work on the railway was being done, with demob uppermost in most people's minds. The last goods coming down the bank from Altenbeken towards Detmold, had somehow become divided, and being piped and braked the two halves had come to a stand. The guard had closed the brake pipe cock on the front portion so that it could set back, but the driver, seeing his brake pressure rise, failed to check what was happening, and rolled on downhill towards Detmold, where the signalman never checked for the tail light to ensure the train was complete, gave "train out of section" to Horn Bad Meinberg, who sent the light engine, off the last passenger working, down towards Detmold. Meanwhile the guard on the freight retired to the warmth of his van, which, fortunately, was not at the back of the train. The light engine came under a bridge and round a curve straight into the back of the goods, splitting one steel coal wagon completely in two longitudinally and severely mauling to or three others, and also derailing a bogie bolster in the middle of the train.

The German breakdown gang was called out and I was to see their efficiency for dealing with such matters. Whereas on British Railways breakdown gangs are volunteers who are on call for such work, the Germans have permanent gangs who live on the train for their period of duty. There were separate gangs, one with a crane and another with jacking equipment, covering quite large areas. In this case, the jacking train came and, used to seeing cranes at most breakdowns I'd been to with Father, I was to see how easily modern lightweight power-operated jacks could do the job.

The breakdown train buffered up to the bottom of the derailed train, and connected up the Westinghouse brake pipes so that there was air pressure on the train. The air-operated hydraulic pump was carried near to the derailed wagon, and connected by its long hose to the train pipe. Lightweight hydraulic jacks were then carried to site, together with good packing. The jacks were connected with high pressure hose, to the hydraulic motor, and the engine's Westinghouse pump did the hard work! The jacks operated upside down, so that when the ram was fully extended, packing was put under a toe on the body so that when pressure was taken off the ram the load was held on the same base packing. The ram retracted by power, packing was put under the head, and up she went again! The jack literally walked up the packing! There were traversing jacks with the traverse power-operated too – I had never realised jacking could be done so quickly, it was not until several years later that the first set of similar equipment was bought by BR "for trial" and has now been universally adopted.

31

This mishap was four days before Christmas 1947. It was a time when the army was changing from its wartime role to Monty's new army, with National Servicemen, but this did not fit in with a unit which was working train services which had to be operated to timetables to suit the commercial requirements of the Reichsbahn.

I took over the loco department from an officer with considerable wartime experience. Many of the older officers were either going on courses, pending staying on for longer in the army, or were attending courses prior to going on demob, and in fact during the early period I was involved with commanding the railway the unit was sometimes reduced to two active officers – the officer Commanding or his deputy in charge of running the camp, and myself, running the railway! Later in the year we got some further young National Service Officers ex Longmoor, and one of them took over the Traffic Department and others were involved on the various administrative jobs.

The Christmas mishap was indicative of the abysmally sloppy operating procedures, and the C.O., Major George Wilkinson, had been put in charge of the unit shortly before my arrival, to endeavour to improve things. He told me that he wanted his loco and traffic officers to get out and about the railway during the hours of darkness. I soon got up in the small hours and appeared at the Shed to take a trip out on one of the early turns. As I subsequently learnt, this was unheard of and caused a veritable panic at all the outstations, with control warning them that I was out on the engine, and all the signalmen were hastily got to work. They just hadn't bothered for a long time, and the trains had just rolled through without taking staffs, and with such German staff as existed working the signals. The very fact that it was known that I was liable to appear at any time was enough to stop the slipshod ways, and I rarely actually disciplined anyone. In any case, we had more subtle ways of dealing with people who could not be trusted when working out on detachment.

The 38 class engines needed careful firing to make them steam properly. We did not get very good coal, and our young National Servicemen were mostly very junior BR footplate staff who had had little or no main line experience. I had to try to encourage them to do the job properly and at the same time try to get the engines themselves into better condition, not easy at a little 'garage' depot dependent upon German staff for all repair work. I tried to introduce a degree of regular manning, particularly with the 38s on the passenger trains, and the lads who were fighting against doing National Service or doing any sort of army activities were weeded out and were given to the RSM for permanent camp duties. In this way we managed to considerably improve our operating performance, and we managed to achieve days when all the trains ran to time.

The 38s had air-operated by-pass valves on the steam chest, which had to be shut before the regulator was opened. It gave a free running engine downhill, but if a Westinghouse pump failed, the engine was a complete failure, though as all trains were air braked this did not really have much consequence. The regulator handle was on a dummy bearing, on the driver's side of the boiler, so that the handle itself was conveniently placed, and was connected by a pair of links to the regulator rod. The engine and tender had straight air brakes which could be used for shunting and also to hold the engine at stops, etc., much as the steam brake can be used on vacuum fitted trains. Turbo generators provided headlights as well as good lighting in the cab to illuminate all the gauges, so different from BR to whom such equipment was a rare novelty, only found on some A1s and B1s, Bulleid Pacifics, etc.

The cab of a 38 class engine. Note regulator linkage.

With only three 38s to meet three passenger diagram workings, it was often necessary to use one of the 50 class 2–10–0s on one or more of them. These engines were fitted with Nicholai valves, a piston valve in two parts, in which steam pressure forces the two halves together to work normally, but when the regulator is closed the heads fall apart allowing free circulation whilst coasting, and avoiding the pumping action which takes place normally. It was necessary, however, to open the regulator gently in order to avoid slamming the heads together and breaking them, a failure which was rather apt to occur, particularly if working on shunting duties. They were however masters of their work, and ran and steamed easily.

Some of the 38s and all of the 50s had feed water heaters. These were excellent fittings if used properly, but it was difficult to get our lads to turn

Nicholai piston valve of a 50 class engine.

on the pump slowly and let it tick away to maintain a steady feed; they were used to injectors, and would work the pump like an injector, turning it full on, filling up the boiler with nearly cold water, then turn it off again. The pumps disliked such treatment and very often stopped working as a result. The injectors were lifting injectors in the cab, on top of the boiler on the 38s, and the mechanical lubricator was similarly in the warm, all to avoid problems in cold and frosty weather. Riding on the engines, I sometimes took the regulator or the shovel and on occasions I managed to roster myself a turn. I became a strong believer in the Westinghouse brake, and endeavoured to master the art of making good smooth stops with it. With the Westinghouse, it is important not to make too many applications as the brake power is exhaustible, relying upon the air stored in the auxiliary reservoirs, and these only fully recharge when the brake handle is put back to 'charge and release', and left there long enough for the full pressure to reach the length of the train. It was, therefore, important not to overbrake, and the aim was to make one application and then partially release it for the final stop, so as not to jerk the train. This was difficult to achieve and needed considerable experience of the stations and the brake power of the train.

Modern air braked stock uses two air pipes so that the auxiliary reservoirs are permanently being charged, and the problem of losing brake power does not then occur. Another problem with the Westinghouse is the freezing of the triple valves, and I learnt this the hard way, one morning when I went out on the first passenger train to Herford. When we got to the first station I applied the brake in the usual way, and little happened; I realised we hadn't much brake power so gave full emergency application, but we sailed through the platform and I had to set back. Fortunately, it was not a manned station – by the military – and it was in effect only a halt, so it didn't matter much, but it was embarassing for me.

On one occasion when we were short of engines we worked the afternoon passenger turn, which was a single trip to Herford, with the two 92 class 0–8–0 tanks, and I worked one of them. On another occasion one of the German 56 class – 56–531 – was being worked through, and I had gone up to Horn Bad Meinberg to meet her. Coming down the bank she dropped a union link pin and bent one of the links, but we got to Detmold and then stripped the motion properly that side, and secured the valve. I made arrangements with Control to give the engine a clear run through to Herford, or, if she *was* stopped, to see she did start before the other train left. I went part of the way with her and jumped off on the move; it was peculiar riding on a single cylinder engine!

Sometimes, when one of our engines had been at Herford for repairs, I would pick it up from Herford Shed, which was a round shed, as usual in Germany. This meant driving the engine out onto the turntable, and as the Germans did not provide any rails opposite, one had to ensure that one stopped properly on the turntable and did not overshoot, or wheels would be off onto the ballast. Anyone who has ever placed a cold superheated engine on a turntable will appreciate the reason for my anxiety; fortunately, being a power turntatble, positioning wasn't too critical, as weight distribution did not matter and there was sufficient length to give a fair margin.

Every afternoon one of the German diesel railcars came through from Bielefeld via Lage to Altenbeken, and then on to Kassel and Frankfurt. There was no balancing northbound working so our tokens slowly migrated south, and the lineman had to periodically adjust staffs by unlocking the instruments, removing an even number of staffs, and putting them into the instrument at the north end of the section.

Detmold Shed was in two parts, a three road "roundhouse" leading on to the turntable, and a two road straight shed, which was chiefly used for the diesels and the four-wheeled railcar and for inspection and repairs. Like all German sheds, there was a tall chimney with connections to the smoke chutes which could be wound down onto the loco chimney both to assist steam raising and to take the smoke right up into the sky, minimising pollution as well as speeding the operation. It was very noticeable how the Germans not only kept the shed clean, but also themselves and in spite of their lack of soap, etc., they all went out of the shed changed and clean. It was difficult to tell labourer from foreman!

Both at Herford and Altenbeken we saw some of the Reichsbahn

The off-centre turntable at Hannover West.

express locos, 01 and 03 Pacifics, including the streamlined 01 class and on one occasion I saw an 05 at Herford, which I managed to photograph.

As I was involved with running the DMR, I did not get the chances to travel around Germany that some of the officers had, but I did get a few opportunities and managed one or two trips on German Pacifics. They ran absolutely like sewing machines with no trace of a knock, they were of course regularly manned as was standard German practice and the driver was responsible for doing all his own minor maintenance. A German driver served two years as a fitter, and the engines were fitted with split and adjustable brasses for virtually everything, so that as wear took place, adjustments could be made to take up any slack.

I spent a week at Hannover at the Railway Control Team Headquarters, the idea being that the officers of the Railway Operating Company should have a greater insight into the general railway organisation in Germany. I was shown Leinhausen Works, and the works shunter, an 0-4-0 with outside Allans straight link motion. Hannover (West) Shed had an interesting arrangement of round houses leading off turntables,

Temporary signal cabin at Nienhagen.

one of which had its arms of unequal length. When an engine needed to be turned round, the short end of the turntable attached itself to a length to bridge the gap, which it took with it as far as required.

To combat the bombing, the Germans had built signal cabins into some of their four-wheeled coaches. To replace a damaged signal cabin, one of these was lifted onto a plinth of sleepers; the signal and point operation was mostly with two wire control so that such an installation could soon be wired up and the blockpost restored to full working conditions.

Whilst at Hannover I went up to Helmstedt to see our Detachment. This was during the blockade when no trains were actually crossing the frontier. It seemed odd to be able to look across the Iron Curtain! One of the bits of nonsense of the Cold War was that the electricity for Helmstedt and surrounding towns was generated at Harbke Power Station, which was in Eastern Germany, across the Iron Curtain.

At Hannover was stored one of the streamline 4–6–4 tanks of Class 61, with 2.3 metre driving wheels. A streamlined tank engine, with the casing nearly down to rail level, it hardly looked like a steam loco!

The journey to and from Detmold – I came home on leave in the middle of the year – was by train to the Hook of Holland, and then night ship to Harwich. Passing through Holland many engines were to be seen showing obvious British parentage, with Beyer Peacock brass beaded splashers and similar features. The Dutch had some Austerities to which they had fitted taller chimneys, making a marked difference to their appearance. The leave trains stopped at Bentheim, the border station, for lunch each way, though there was a NAAFI buffet car on the train for tea, etc. It was a very comfortable and pleasant journey to make.

348 gave up operating the DMR in September 1948, but with the Berlin blockade, etc., there was a three months deferment of demob, so that we suddenly found ourselves with a lot of people who we had to keep usefully occupied. Then it was said that the deferred people would be home by Christmas, and my demob came through for the day on which we were having the dress rehearsal for a production of the Mikado! When I learnt the news I was not too pleased, and it was arranged that I could not be released until after 31st December, when the unit was officially disbanding. When I did go on demob, it was realised that I had been released from a unit that did not exist, so some paperwork had to be hastily redone! I went from Detmold to Bielefeld where I was given a draft of demob-happy soldiers to bring across and take to York. I was very pleased to get

Class 61 streamlined 4–6–4 tank engine.

38

to York with them and hand them, and their papers, over to the demob unit, pick up my civvy suit and get to the station in time to catch the York – Colchester at 3.15pm, as I knew that if I missed that I'd got a slow and arduous journey via Retford.

Lt. Allan Garraway, with Sgt. Street, outside Detmold Loco offices.

CHAPTER IV

Doncaster

From my earliest childhood, railways have always been my main interest, and I had always hoped to follow in Father's footsteps. When I was about 16, Father sought advice from Edward Thompson, Chief Mechanical Engineer of the LNER, regarding the best training for the locomotive side of the LNER and, as a Cambridge man, he had told Father to get me to University first. Thompson also said that he and the LMS people were discussing ways of training professional engineers coming back from the War, and thought that possibly I would fit into such a scheme. He also gave Father a letter confirming the discussion, as he expected to have retired when the time came. When I went into the army, Father mentioned the matter to Peppercorn who had by then succeeded Thompson as CME, and as soon as I came home from Germany, we arranged to go to Doncaster to see him. Nationalisation had by then taken place, and with it the first wave of centralisation and standardisation, and Peppercorn told us that as far as he was concerned, I could start straight away, but under the new regime he hadn't the authority, and would have to refer the matter to H.Q., i.e. Marylebone.

Meanwhile, I was also trying to get into the Royal Engineers Supplementary Reserve, which was then being reformed, and I had an interview with the C.O., Colonel Thomas, who was P.R. and P.O. for the Eastern Region, based at Marylebone. He accepted me for 157 Loco Running Squadron, subject to my being accepted onto British Rail, and he found out and told me that it had been agreed for me to go to Doncaster, before I heard officially via Doncaster itself!

In due course, I was told that I had been accepted for Doncaster, and that I would be paid the princely sum of 99/6d. per week. This compared with two of my confederates from Longmoor days, who joined the Railway as traffic apprentices and started as salaried staff in grade 2 at £450 per year, all counting towards pensions, etc., so it was not surprising that Engineers in those days completely ignored BR as a career. Subsequently, BR realised that they had got to attract young professional engineers, and the training devised was very similar to that which I had done, but with salaried status just the same as other professional trainees.

I duly reported to Doncaster in March 1949, and was introduced to C.F. Rose, the Assistant Loco Works Manager, who was to look after my problems and needs. A programme was devised for me giving periods in all the main parts of the Loco Works, but it did not include any time in the carriage works, which was in so many ways a completely different empire.

The first two months I spent in the pattern shop. Whilst I found the work interesting, it was work which required a high degree of woodworking skill as well as knowledge of foundry work, and I was not able to get very much involved. Pattern makers were the most highly rated craftsmen in the Works, though with piece work that did not make them the highest paid. Work which I found particularly enjoyable was the making of patches for cracked cylinders, etc., done by making a brass casting for the patch, for which a pattern was made, usually out of plaster. A wooden box was made to fit around the area concerned, which had to be sealed tight to the casting, and then plaster was poured into the box. After the plaster had set, and had been carefully removed, the plaster cast was trimmed and prepared ready for the foundry. Apart from the fact that the work had to be done away from the pattern shop, it involved liaison with the fitting staff who would subsequently fit it, so that there was sufficient space for fastening, etc. John Brooks, who usually did this work, was an old Sapper, and I got on well with him, so that I was able to go about the Works with him and got to know a number of people, as well as join with him in doing the work. After the patch was cast in the brass shop, fitters then secured it to the cylinder with rows of set screws, which had to be carefully drilled and tapped, all a laborious process. Finally it was all bolted up with a liberal coating of red lead as jointing. If everything went all right, the patch fitted snugly, but sometimes it distorted slightly in being cast and the fitter had a job to make the patch fit snugly into the broken casting.

As was logical, I followed this with a spell in both the iron and brass foundries. I got opportunities to help in making moulds, cores, etc., which made the stay more interesting as it was part of the Works which ordinary apprentices never visited and of which, consequently, they had no experience. Then I moved to the blacksmiths and fabrication shop and I was fortunate in becoming friendly with one of the welders, who taught me the art on odd bits of scrap, and then let me do some of the simpler welds. Engine and tender rubbing blocks were a favourite task not requiring high standards, and I was able to get valuable practice in welding, as well as learning something of the problems.

The normal Premium Apprentices were part of the production teams of the Works, and worked in the various gangs with the fitters and were expected to contribute to the output of the gangs. I gained useful experience in a wider range of activities than they did, but lost the opportunities to gain practical experience as a craftsman. Nevertheless, where I found someone who would give me jobs, and they realised that I liked actually working and had some idea as to how to handle tools, they found me jobs to do which gave me useful experience. When I first went to 'D' shop, I found myself watching machinists at work, so I went to the foreman and told him that I wanted to gain some practical experience like the Premium Apprentices. He told me that for someone who had been to University, I

Doncaster Pattern Shop.

should learn all I needed to know by watching, but he did eventually allow me to join the apprentice gang in B1 Shop, making brake hanger bolts, etc.

The last of the LNER designed A1s were being built at that time, and I did some work on the main frames and bogies and other components for them. The cylinders for the 4MT 2–6–0s which was Doncaster's next order for new construction, were coming in for machining; being steel, these were a new departure for Doncaster, and I spent some time on the boring machine with them, learning at first hand the short life of the boring tool when working on a steel casting as against an iron casting.

In due course I went to the Crimpsall Shops, which concentrated on engine repairs. This was more or less a complete complex of its own, some distance away at the west of the Works, doing virtually everything for engine repairs, but any new components, such as cylinders or any other part would be made and machined in the main part of the Works. On the other hand, tyres were fitted to wheel centres, wheels fitted to axles, and quartered and balanced in 'Q' shop, which was part of Crimpsall, for new engines as well as repairs. I saw the roller bearing axles being assembled for the batch of five A1s so fitted, the axles being machined on lathes of great age.

To start with I spent time on the bench repairing valve gear and valves, and then I had a very enjoyable short spell finishing off the repairs to the Doncaster Carr Loco 45-ton crane and assisting with testing it in steam. I virtually taught myself how to fire and drive it as was needed by those working to finish its repairs.

4 Bay was where the Pacifics and V2s were reassembled. The bare frames came in at the top end and the first job was to set up the frame assembly level. If frames were bent they would be straightened by peening with a pneumatic hammer. Sometimes frames would be cracked, in which case the crack, if small, would be chipped out and welded. Often a half moon shaped area would be cut out over the horns where cracking usually took place, and a new piece of plate would be welded into position. Sometimes a complete new front end would be welded onto the frames – this was done for the 'bastard' A1 – 60113, and I managed to photograph the job during the lunch break. The folding Voigtlander which I had got whilst in Germany, for which I had a soft leather pouch, would fit in my trouser pocket, which enabled me to photograph many interesting happenings and arrivals, etc. during my stay at the Works. The camera got laid on and squeezed when climbing into boilers through domes, etc., but it still works very well!

After the frames had been trued up, the horns would be refitted, as necessary, and then the horn faces would be ground and filed so that they were square across the engine, and the correct distance from one horn to the next. Cylinders might have new bolts fitted, if required, and would be rebored, depending upon their condition. When this had all been completed, the assembly was then normally moved down the shop for the boiler to be put on, followed by the cab and all the pipework and details, and the whole wheeled. The valve gear and connecting rods would be put up for valve setting, a subject dear to my heart, and I enjoyed myself working under Arthur Turner in his gang. The valves for two engines, 60080 and 60068 I completely set myself, and I still have the complete set of actual readings that were obtained, which have subsequently proved of help to Bill Harvey when resetting valves for *Flying Scotsman* at Carnforth.

Examiners looked at the engines as they came in for repairs, and decided what work was necessary for each engine. The difference in the

Plate for new front end frames for 60113 Great Northern.

boiler condition of the Haymarket engines, on soft Scottish water, as against the King's Cross engines on hard water, was very noticeable, and I found this very salutary. At this time Doncaster was changing to the LMS system of heavy intermediate repairs where the boiler was left in the frames. This was relatively straightforward with Pacifics and V2s, with their wide fireboxes sitting above the frames, but it didn't quite fit into the traditional methods of the Crimpsall, and tended to disrupt the flow of work.

From 4 Bay the engines went to the paint shop, and then back to the weigh house where the boilers were filled, the engines tested in steam and the springs adjusted. During the week I spent there I attained the ambition of most apprentices and went on trial to Barkston Triangle, north of Grantham, with 60100 and 60092. These runs gave the engines a quiet trip of about ninety miles light engine before going back to Doncaster Carr Loco and working back to their home depot, and an opportunity to find any faults, in which case these were dealt with.

After 4 Bay I went to the new Erecting Shop where construction of the LMS designed Class 4 2–6–0s was in progress. This Shop was intended for new construction work, but when not thus occupied, engines for repairs were brought in. It was not laid out for the dirty work of stripping engines and overhauling bits and pieces, but for erecting clean new components,

44

New front end frames for 60113 after welding and profiling.

delivered from 'D' shop. From my diary, I note that 43069 was the engine which seems to have had some attention from me.

My final spell was spent in the boiler shop seeing how plates were rolled and flanged to form the various components which were then drilled and rivetted to make fireboxes and boilers. It was interesting to see large-scale application of that drawing office problem on development of surfaces and to see the way in which experts juggled with rolling the plate to form the various sections, though it was also interesting to note the "strong arm" methods sometimes used to force recalcitrant bits together when something hadn't gone exactly right.

During those last weeks of my allocated time, I was making overtures that I wanted to go to the Motive Power Department for some practical experience. I hoped ultimately to go permanently onto this side of the business, and I definitely did not want to remain in the Works or the Drawing Office. By that time, Peppercorn had retired and J.F. Harrison, who did not have such a good relationship with L.P. Parker, the Motive Power Superintendent of the Eastern Region had taken over. He, therefore, arranged for me to spend the last two and a half months of my two years under F.H. Petty in the North Eastern Region Motive Power Department, and on New Year's Day I reported to York. There was no holiday for the New Year in those days, and Christmas was only a two day affair which always meant returning to Doncaster, or wherever, on Boxing Day evening, ready to start work first thing on the 27th.

I reported to Mr. Mathewson Dick, DMPS at York, who decided that I should spend most of my time at Leeds Neville Hill Depot, so I occupied the rest of the day having a look at York Shed and the old Queen Street Railway Museum before returning to Doncaster. I had by then, after various not so happy experiences, got very good lodgings in Thorne Road, and with the uncertainties for the future, preferred to stay there. It was easy to commute from Doncaster to Leeds, and then travel out to Neville Hill on the tram. If I saw one of the ex-London 'Feltham' trams coming, I always tried to catch it; the route went onto a reserved central reservation on the city outskirts, and I enjoyed the way those trams would go when they had the chance on the stretch before I had to get off. Normally going home I rode up to Leeds City on a light engine before catching a train home from Central.

Once again, a programme had been mapped out for me, to spend various periods with the different sections of activity, starting with the Running Foreman on the various shifts. It was a joy to be in a shed and away from the regular hours of the Works, and working nights gave me opportunities to travel to and from Leeds by various roundabout routes as I had been given a pass for "all stations in Yorkshire".

When I was working with the fitters, they had a problem with 60081. The North Eastern sheds did not set valves in the way to which I was accustomed, i.e. by quartering the wheels and equalising leads, with appropriate expansion allowances, but were used to using "standard plates". These were templates with the correct readings on them, one template being clamped to the valve spindle, the other to one of the cover studs. The valve was then adjusted so that the readings coincided. I never saw one used, but whilst it had some merits in simplicity, if any part of the valve gear was slightly out, and few engines are 100 per cent correct, there was not the same opportunity for analysing the problem. I told them I was quite willing to try to set 60081s valves in the Doncaster manner, and next morning I called into the Crimpsall and saw Arthur Turner, who lent and gave me various of his trammels and gauges, and I got the Neville Hill blacksmith to make up a similar set. I then marked off the spindles before the valves were put back, and when the engine was fully assembled set the

46

valves throughout using the same Doncaster expansion allowances. How-ever, whereas in Crimpsall we had the driving wheels on rollers, which were turned over by an electric motor which could be started, stopped and reversed at will (the side rods were not put on for valve setting), in the running shed we had to get a gang with pinch bars to move the engine up and down, and it was obviously essential to do things right first time!

On Pacifics and V2s with the 2 to 1 gear in front of the cylinders, it was necessary to set the middle valve from the back cover, which necessitated standing on top of the bogie, keeping clear of the gudgeon pin and its split pin as it scraped past one's chest. In the Works there were electric hand lamps, the engine was stationary, and movement of the wheels were con-trolled by an electric motor, but in a running shed the engine was moving by jerks, and just as the mark was appearing against the trammel, I would find that I was being dragged by the crosshead, whose split pin had just caught in my overalls! Neville Hill was one of the depots where the fitters *would* use miners' lamps; these were a great asset, though many people would not use them, complaining of the weight of the batteries held on a waist belt. When I started working at Boston Lodge, where there was no electricity, I got a similar lamp from the Nife people. It has been over-hauled once, but still works well and holds its charge, after thirty years.

Setting ex-LNER engine valves was a great deal easier than LMS engines, as the valve spindle end was parallel, and its relationship to the valve crosshead was adjusted by putting in or taking out 'buttons' from between the spindle end and the bottom of the crosshead hole. These 'buttons' were round discs of varying thicknesses made from plate, the thinner ones being cut out by tin snips. After getting the correct thickness of buttons the cotter would have to be properly fitted with its own cotter tight up to the valve crosshead.

On Saturday, 24th February, I rode with 60081 from Neville Hill through Harrogate and Ripon to Darlington, and everyone was delighted with the improvement in her performance. My success with this little job gave me an introduction to the old experienced hands which was extremely useful; I had gone to learn from them, yet had started by helping them with a problem!

Subsequently, I set the valves on a J39 and was involved with steaming problems with some of the B1s but I finished with a short spell at District Office at York where I was given the job of looking at the new 4MT class engines ex-Doncaster and I spent a few days riding on two or three and going to the sheds to find out the problems with them. It also gave me an insight into the different organisation of the North Eastern Region, whereby the small sheds were under the supervision of the Station Master, who would, nevertheless, have a considerable amount of loco experience. The old North Eastern Railway had remained an independent area under the LNER and a separate region under BR, and it had retained quite a lot of its old traditions and ways.

The end of my two year period was approaching and I had made it clear where I wanted to go. At that time the Eastern and North Eastern regions still had the old LNER practice of young men working as supernumaries in the Motive Power Department, either in Grade 3 as Supernumary Running Foremen' or in Grade 2 as 'Mechanical Foremen (Learner)'. The North Eastern Region already had their full establishment of the latter, but as there were vacancies at York Shed for fitters, Mr. Mathewson Dick told me he would be pleased to have me in the York District Office, though paid as a fitter, which I was pleased to accept. Just as I had finished my report on the 4 MTs, I got word that the great Mr. L.P. Parker at Liverpool Street had offered me a post as a Grade 2 Mechanical Foreman (Learner) at Stratford. I was, of course, delighted and went off down there on the Monday to start work with T.C.B. Miller, DMPS, as one of LPPs 'young men'. Dick Hardy, in "Steam in the Blood", writes about the great Leslie Preston Parker, one of the real characters of the LNER and Eastern Region, and I am very pleased that I worked under him for his last few years. A martinet in many ways, feared by many, yet when the time came for him to retire, it was very noticeable how everyone was sorry to see him go.

Typical of him was the letter he wrote to Father. "Mr. Harrison asked me a week or so back whether there was any capacity in which I could provide some more Motive Power experience for a young man named A.G.W. Garraway, recited his qualifications, and asked if I would like to see him. In view of the distinguished ancestry which I deduced from the candidate's surname, I told Mr. Harrison that I could fit this young man into a Mechanical Learner Grade 2 post immediately, leaving the interview until he arrived." Father replied, thanking LPP, though feeling that probably one Garraway in the Eastern Region was quite sufficient! Father made the point that once he had started me at Doncaster he did not want to interfere and wanted me to find my own way in the world. He concluded by saying that I had gone up to Stratford that day, looking forward to my new work and associating in the scenes of his youth, with great eagerness.

I never actually had that interview, though of course, had many meetings and discussions with LPP in his office whilst working in various sections of the offices.

CHAPTER V

1951 –
Festival of Britain:
Britannias and a job in the
Motive Power Department

Stratford was the largest loco depot in the world and was also the home of the Great Eastern Locomotive Works. However, my stay there was brief, just over a month spent mostly in trying to get the new BR planned maintenance scheme operating at the small sub sheds around the District (as laid down in a document known as MP11 which set out schedules of examination). It was the period when the first of the new BR standard steam locos were arriving from Crewe, and to me, though I did not of course realise it at the time, included an event which was to subsequently radically change my career. Bill Harvey, Shed Master from Norwich, came up to find out about the Britannias before he received his first example. At Stratford, the officers usually had lunch at one of the cafes or hostelries in Stratford Market Place. I went to Dick Robsons office, the Shed Master, and he suggested we took Bill Harvey for a superior lunch at the "Two Puddings". During the course of discussing holiday plans, Bill mentioned that he was arranging to go to Towyn to work in the workshops of the Talyllyn Railway which had just been taken over by a Society. I said that I had just joined the Society and was thinking about going to Towyn, but had not made any firm arrangements. He booked me in with him where he was staying, and so started not only a close personal association, but also my connections with Welsh Railways.

One of the outstations which I arranged to visit, though not strictly for business, was Kelvedon, the junction of the Kelvedon and Tollesbury Light Railway. I had visited the line from Cambridge in the early days of the war, but it was a line to fall under the closure axe on 5th May 1951. Its passenger trains were mixed, and its passengers were carried in special coaches fitted with verandahs which the GER had originally built for the Wisbech and Upwell tramway.

One of them was used in the film "Titfield Thunderbolt" and should have been preserved, but Stratford Works somehow forgot. The branch

An ageing J15 on a Kelvedon and Tollesbury mixed train, just before the line was closed in May 1951.

was virtually an independent line, ideal for a preservation scheme today, with its own station and small engine shed at ground level, the main line station being on top of an embankment. There was, of course, a connecting spur between the two lines. It was normally worked by one of the GER 0–6–0 tanks, or a J15, as it was a very lightly laid line over which only the lightest engines could run.

Another oddity was Epping. This had been one of the small sub depots for working the Liverpool Street suburban services, but with the Central Line electrification it should have been closed. However, although the third and fourth rails had been laid through to Ongar, the future of this line had still not been decided. In fact, my first job at Liverpool Street meant I periodically had to answer questions from the accountants, and others, on this branch, sometimes in connection with the proposed closure and at other times with its electrification. When I suggested that it would be more sensible to consider the two things

The Ongar push-pull train and a Central line tube train at Epping.

together, I was agreed with, but was told to just get on with answering the questions! In the interim the Epping-Ongar spur was worked as a virtually isolated outpost by steam push and pull, the shed being closed and the engine provided by Stratford, going out and in over the Central Line tracks.

The Great Eastern main line to Norwich via Ipswich even in LNER days had never had anything larger than moderate 4–6–0s, B12s, B17s and then B1s, due to weight restrictions, but the new Britannias were to go to Norwich and Stratford to work a completely recast hourly service between Liverpool Street and Norwich, with the fastest trains doing the run in two hours. The heavy Hook Continental Boat Train was also included in the speed up programme, and was a priority for Britannia haulage. Unfortunately, the service was planned to be introduced before sufficient of the engines were built, coupled with the fact that one was in the Festival Exhibition on the South Bank in London, and so the Southern provided two small Pacifics, *Hurricane* and *Boscastle* to assist. These were strange engines for the GE men, also they did not have water scoops and, consequently, had to take water at Ipswich. I did look into the possibility of fitting LNER Group Standard tenders to them – I still have my report on the subject – and although it was practicable, the new Britannias, aided by the good B1s managed to sustain the service and the Southern Pacifics spent a lot of their time working on the Cambridge line.

My first spell at Liverpool Street was with the Utilisation Section. This dealt with the operating side of the Motive Power Department, engine allocations to depots, engine working arrangements, etc., though the detailed engine diagrams were prepared by a special section of the Operating Department. It also included the loco inspectors at HQ, including Sam Jenkins, Len Theobald and Bert Dixon. Sam Jenkins was a stalwart of the GN main line, who could tell stories of many of the famous exploits on which he was the inspector, including the pre-war Silver Jubilee and Coronation high-speed runs. Len Theobald was a Great Eastern man and concentrated mostly on that section, whilst Bert Dixon was younger and covered everywhere, and I am pleased to say that in his retirement in East Anglia he continues to take an interest in steam.

On the Eastern Region at that time there were several young men, as Leslie Parker termed his supernumary engineers, including John Bellwood, now CME at the National Railway Museum, York. The MP Department was working eleven day fortnights, so we worked alternate Saturday mornings. John and some of the others came from Yorkshire, and on Friday afternoons there were usually enquiries of Kings Cross Top Shed as to the driver and engine on the 5.30 pm "Yorkshire Pullman". Sometimes, if two of them were going down on the same Friday evening, they both assisted the fireman. Whilst working at HQ, we all had footplate passes for the Eastern Motive Power Area, which we used to the full; Liverpool Street was still responsible for operating the Great Central

Boscastle *on arrival at Stratford, on 8th May 1951.*

line, from Marylebone to Manchester, though most of it was in the LM Region, as well as to Leeds and Bradford, which were in the NE region, but, conversely, Liverpool Street had little jurisdiction over Sheffield Midland, etc.

Actually, I was not very interested in having Saturday mornings off as, soon after I got to London, I had made contact with the Oakley Rowing Club, which was a section of the GN Athletic Association, a sports and social club formed originally by the GN for its staff, with its main base at Gordon Hill. It was becoming part of the then newly-formed BR Staff Association. I wanted to keep up the sport I had started at Cambridge, which I thoroughly enjoyed, and pursued a little in Germany, but did not want to get too tied down with training programmes and complete dedication, which would have been necessary if I had got involved with serious competitive activities. We were a jolly little crowd, based at Hammersmith with little connection with Gordon Hill, and we just managed to raise an VIII to enter the Head of the River Race each year. Although my Cambridge rowing had all been on bow side, Oakley not only made me row on stroke side but also row as stroke itself. In the summer we got out on one or two evenings a week, but always on Saturday afternoons, so that my usual train home was the 6.18pm Kings Cross – Leeds train, which was a Copley Hill A1 with Kings Cross no.2 link men, and usually I travelled on the engine.

1951 was a bad year on the East Coast main line for timekeeping. After the war the LMS practice of through engine workings had been adopted, where an engine started at, say, Kings Cross with one set of men and then various sets took over at different points en route, as is done today with diesels and electrics. With modern motive power this is perfectly satisfactory, but to give its best performance a steam loco depends on the skill of the driver and fireman. Above all, when engines are running around all over the country, they become nobody's baby and by the time they eventually get back to their home depot, they have become thoroughly neglected, and work correspondingly. It all came to a head one day when the engine for the 2.00pm "Heart of Midlothian" had failed, and King's Cross had not got an engine to take the train, which finally left an hour late. There was naturally, quite a row about it, so Leslie Parker put his foot down and said that whilst through engine workings might be more economical in a perfect world, in those times, with varying standards of coal available, it was necessary to adapt the workings to suit the circumstances. It was found that it was possible to re-diagram the main line express workings so that most men could work their shift with the same engine from their own depot. Grantham again became an engine changing point, for which they were given A1s which they were able to keep to two sets of men. In fact, there were some engines and men that stayed together until the diesel era. A few trains changed engines at Peterborough, which had A2s. The A4s were concentrated at King's Cross, and the top link again had them regularly manned, though with the lodging jobs to Newcastle and Leeds, and the summer non-stops, the

A view from the top corridor window of Hamilton House, with Liverpool Street station in the foreground, Broad Street signal box behind and above.

associations could not be so close. Copley Hill had A1s but insufficient workings to keep them regularly manned, but they did have their own depots engines on the more important workings, which they worked out and home, including the up and down Queen of Scots Pullman and the up and down Leeds "flyer" 7.50 am out of King's Cross in the morning and the 6.20 pm up from Leeds which were lodging turns also, and the 10.45 am Leeds to King's Cross and 3.50 pm down. The A3s were distributed for the less important workings, according to needs. In this way, each depot was primarily maintaining its own stock and if their engines failed it reacted far more on them, so that both maintenance staff and engine crews were encouraged to do their best for their own depot's reputation, and weren't struggling with other people's neglected engines.

During this spell at LV (which was the code for Liverpool Street Headquarters), I had one or two trips out on the Southern engines temporarily at Stratford. They were also used for two days on special test runs to Norwich via Ely, with specially relaxed speed restrictions, and I was one of those recording speeds and times. This was partly in connection with the complete revamping of the Cambridge line to integrate the Britannia workings between the Cambridge and Ipswich lines and improve the service. The performance was good by Cambridge line standards, and speeds of up to the seventies were achieved, which was the maximum allowed. On the first day, Thursday, 27 September, with 12 bogies, the train only stopped for water at Ely, but on the second day it stopped at principal stations to Ely, detached six coaches, and then stopped at all stations to Norwich, similarly in the reverse direction.

The new Britannias were very much under the eye of everyone, from all aspects, and they were tested not only on the Rugby Testing Plant, but also with the Dynamometer Cars. The LNER car was used for some trials to Harwich, and it was arranged for me to travel down in it. There was no opportunity for any very startling performance on such a run, and in fact I have little recollection of the trip, apart from the interest of seeing the car at work.

In the autumn I was moved to the Plaistow District. This was the old London Tilbury & Southend Section which the Midland had pinched from under the nose of the GER, and on nationalisation had finally been put under the rightful control of Liverpool Street. It was an exceedingly compact and self-contained little district, but of course it was organised very much on LMS practices, though as more Eastern Region staff went to it, LNER methods were introduced. Essentially, it was a passenger railway with an intensive surburban service for commuters, up in the morning, down in the evening. Freight came in via Woodgrange Park from the GE lines and the LMS mostly going to Fords at Dagenham and Tilbury Docks. There was also a little local freight coming in off the North London at Bow to Bromley, and the GE Woolwich branch at Abbey Mills. Plaistow was the District Office, presided over by Geoffrey Ford, whom I had known from Cambridge days, when he had been Shed Master at Bury St. Edmunds. Plaistow was the main depot for the district, the concentration depot, as it was known by the LMS, and all washouts, examinations and main repairs were done there. The two garage depots, at Tilbury and Shoeburyness, were only for stabling and had no facilities for repairs other than for day to day servicing.

The loco fleet consisted mostly of Class 4 2–6–4 tanks, including virtually all the three cylinder 2500s. There were various versions of the two cylinder Class 4 tanks, from the Fowler engines, which were not liked, to the latest Ivatt engines. A few of the old Tilbury Class 3 4–4–2 tanks remained, as well as Tilbury 0–6–2 tanks for local freight workings, and some J17s had been introduced for freight workings to replace Midland 0–6–0s.

The working of the section typified the cost of working commuter services. Basically, there was an hourly service of both fast and slow trains to Southend, and Shoeburyness, and an hourly slow train to Pitsea via Tilbury, which ran throughout the day in both directions. For the morning rush hour, Shoeburyness engines and men (and some from Tilbury) brought trains up to Fenchurch Street, worked empty coaches to Barking carriage sidings, and then went Light Engine to Plaistow Shed, the crew returning to Tilbury or Shoeburyness 'on the cushions'. In the afternoon another crew came up to Plaistow on the cushions, prepared the engine, went to Barking for coaches, took them to Fenchurch Street, worked a load of commuters back home, put coaches and engine away, and booked off. In other words, each commuter train, complete with engine, worked one round trip each day, for which it required two crews.

Obviously, in practice some of the regular interval trains integrated into the rush hour trains, but there were a lot of engines which came into Plaistow each day from Shoeburyness and Tilbury, and sets of carriages likewise, which did no revenue service other than the one round trip per day. It did however provide a ready means of changing engines over for wash out, examination, etc.

The three cylinder engines were based on Shoeburyness, and were mostly manned by regular men. Five engines at Tilbury, 2218 to 2222, were also regularly manned, and some at Plaistow. These men took great pride in their regular engines, naturally some more so than others, but they all kept their cabs clean, with tool lockers tidy, newspaper on shelves in the clothing cupboard, and the boiler front clean and bright. Some took great pride in polishing their pipework and fittings, which the commuters noticed and commented upon as they walked past at Fenchurch Street. The fireirons were kept chained and padlocked, which avoided the problem of loss, which was one of the causes of engines being late off shed, and the tool and clothing cupboards were padlocked, the keys being on a ring with a large tin label with the engine number, which the fireman drew from the Stores. These regular engines were all well equipped with all the necessary tools, hammers and lamps, which were properly looked after and worked. This was all part of the magic of having engines regularly manned, wherever it was done, and many crews would spend time at terminii, etc., giving the cabs and everything else that little bit of extra attention which made work more pleasant for them and more efficient for the railway. Moreover, they made sure that minor defects were put right before they became a major fault or caused a failure.

I am very pleased that 2500 has been preserved, as part of the National Collection, at time of writing located at Bressingham, as it was to my mind one of the best designs of passenger tank engine there have been. They ran like sewing machines, and rode well. Although a run of forty miles to Shoeburyness isn't far, it was not a flat line, with a climb from Pitsea to Laindon and a drop then to Upminster. The trains were non-corridor sets of 11 coaches, which carried a fair number of people, so weighed heavily in the rush hour, and there was no time for hanging around. In the rush hours the trains ran fairly closely nose to tail, particularly between Fenchurch Street and Barking, so if one engine was doing badly, it would upset the whole service.

At times of engine shortage, the Tilbury Class 3s had to deputise and these were very hard pressed to manage; they were kept out of the rush hour and used on the lighter workings as far as possible. Occasionally, they got onto a fast Southend express. One of their features was that they were fitted with power reversers like the Southern Pacifics and some NE engines, etc. Nearly all power reversers had the fault that the gear crept, and was difficult to adjust. It always seemed to me that the object of power reversers was lost. Power reversing is needed when shunting, where the engine is continually being reversed, but on main line engines a screw reverser is needed so that small adjustments can be made. Power reversers are normally held in position by water in a cylinder, but this always leaks slightly, allowing the cut off to vary. I could never understand why the power reverse of the GE could not have been adapted and more widely used. The GE, being a Westinghouse braked line, used air for its power reverse, as well as operating its water scoops and sanding gear, but it also had a screw reverser for small adjustments when running, of which the nut was a half nut similar to what is used on a lathe leadscrew. The illustration of the arrangement, taken from GER Instructions of 1914 shows the small lever which operated the valves which admitted air to the power cylinder, and at the same time disengaged the half nut. When the gear had moved to where it was wanted, the lever was put to the mid position, so that air was admitted to both sides of the operating cylinder, and the half nut re-engaged with the screw, so that there were all the advantages of power reverse for shunting, with the screw reverse available for use on the run. One of the Class 3 PTs, *Thundersley* is also at Bressingham, and the arrangement of the reverser in the cab can be seen as an example of how not to arrange things. There is the power cylinder nearest the bunker, and the water cylinder to lock the gear against the boiler, with a crosshead and connection onto the bridle rod between. To change the cup leathers in the water cylinder was a major dismantling job which, therefore, did not get done, so that when the gear started to slip drivers wedged it with any convenient object, very often a fishplate bolt which happened to be just the right size. Sometimes drivers got their fingers mixed up with the bolt, and there were many men on the LT & S section without some of their fingers. It was a lethal piece of apparatus, and Bill Harvey has protected it on *Thundersley* so that today's engine crews do not get themselves tangled up in it.

When I moved to Plaistow, Liverpool Street told me to keep my footplate pass until it was due for renewal at the end of the year. However, the Chief Clerk at Plaistow, a very officious ex LMS individual, told me I was no longer entitled to it and made me give it up to him. Next day I mentioned what had happened to Geoff Ford, the DMPS and he was very

DIAGRAM OF POWER REVERSING GEAR

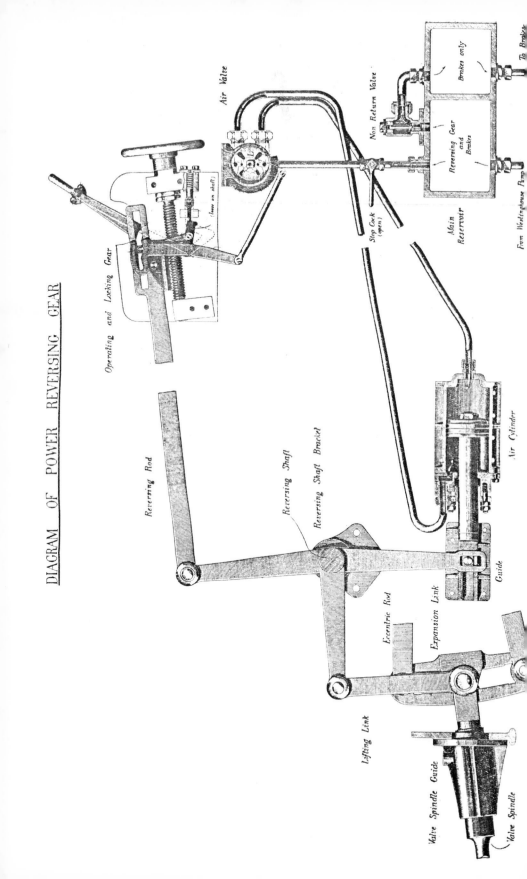

Air Valve

Operating and Locking Gear

(loose on shaft)

Non Return Valve

Brakes only

To Brakes

Reversing Gear and Brakes

Main Reservoir

From Westinghouse Pump

Stop Cock (open)

Reversing Rod

Reversing Shaft

Reversing Shaft Bracket

Air Cylinder

Guide

Eccentric Rod

Expansion Link

Lifting Link

Valve Spindle Guide

Valve Spindle

cross, especially when he found that it had been actually sent to London not under his signature. I told him that I always rode up on the engine on Sunday nights and would prefer to do it legally, so he mentioned the matter to L.P. Parker, who said that my pass would also include King's Cross to Lincoln, as he liked his young men to gain as much experience as possible. A sequel with that Chief Clerk gave several of us some quiet amusement! Both the shed master and district boiler foreman were also living in digs, and had been home for the Christmas Holiday. The day after Boxing Day we were all back in the office first thing, since we had travelled back the previous evening, and Geoff Ford was quite cross with us for not travelling back first thing in the morning, as we all enjoyed a lot of personal freedom because we were prepared to give and take. When he rang for his Chief Clerk, who also lived away, one of the relatively junior clerks came in, as the second clerk was on holiday and the Chief Clerk was not back. Geoff was livid! Words were obviously said, as on the Chief Clerk's next long weekend, he got back into the office in the early hours and had a snooze there, instead of coming back mid-morning, as had been his practice.

During my spell on the Tilbury section I spent quite a lot of time actually at Tilbury. This was the smallest of the three depots of the District, with a Shed Master who, as at Shoeburyness, also acted as day shift running foreman. Tilbury Riverside Station was a terminus ending up at the pier where ships loaded their passengers; many years later when we went on a cruise to the Canaries, we joined the ship at Tilbury from that very pier. At the platform ends, one line went left to Tilbury Town Station, for Barking, and the main line to London, whereas the other arm went east to Pitsea, where it joined the main line through Upminster to Southend.

There was a third side to the triangle, enabling the freight trains from Thames Haven Refinery to run from east to west, and inside the triangle was the depot. It consisted of a large through shed, in a deplorable state, with one of the small skip type coaling plants, a water tank, with a small office and oil store underneath. As a garage depot it only needed facilities for servicing and stabling engines, and all except simple day to day repairs were done when the engines went to Plaistow.

The condition of the sheds themselves at Tilbury and Shoeburyness were terrible, but not altogether untypical of the conditions under which people were expected to service and maintain steam locos. One day I was at Tilbury and Geoff Ford, the DMPS, telephoned and asked me to take some photos – he knew I usually carried my camera with me – as some questions had been asked at high level on the subject. Tilbury shed was a vast barn and a rare instance where the shed was larger than necessary, but it faced east so the winds blew straight up the Thames estuary and through the shed, which was never very full. Shoeburyness shed was beside the passenger station but in an even more deplorable state. I photographed Tilbury, then went to Shoeburyness, and Bill Harper, the Shed Master, took me up on the water tank and onto the planks over the

Part of Shoeburyness shed roof.

water to take the photos. It was a very windy day, I don't like heights and I was not at all happy taking the photos, especially as I had to wait whilst some of the smoke and steam cleared! I don't think much was ever done to the Shed before electrification and the end of steam, but day to day jobs and daily examinations had to be done in it as well as enginemen doing their oiling and preparation.

The Class 3 tanks were mostly used on the Tilbury line trains, but also as standby when there was a shortage of Class 4s. When handled by the older Tilbury men, they would do the job perfectly well. 1952, 1969, 1975, 1977 and 1993 all appear in my diary. Tilbury worked few of the faster Shoeburyness trains, but did work the 7.00 pm ex Fenchurch Street at the end of the evening rush which was first stop Upminster, then Leigh and all stations to Shoeburyness, and to my knowledge on at least one night when the booked Class 4 failed at Tilbury the spare engine was a Class 3, which worked the job without losing time. As I spent much of my time at Tilbury, I got to know some of the regular drivers, particularly on 2218 and 2220, and when possible I travelled with them in the evening and often either drove or fired. Working local trains is very good practice in working the brake, and to keep time with the trains it was important not only to stop in the right place, but with a rising brake; in other words, with the vacuum recreating, so that not only did the passengers have a more comfortable ride through a gentle final stop, but also the brakes were nearly off as the train stopped, so that it was possible to get away quickly immediately the guard gave the right away. I enjoyed those evenings very much, and it was valuable experience.

The Thames estuary was very liable to fog, and to help the working of the trains and to aid safety, the engines were all fitted with the Hudd system of Automatic Train Control, as it was then known, Automatic Warning System as it is more logically called today.

This was the forerunner to the BR system, and relied on magnets in the middle of the track actuating magnets in a receiver on the engine. On the approach to a signal, the first track magnet was a permanent magnet, which operated the engine magnet to open a small air valve in the engine receiver which caused an air siren to sound in the cab. The second track magnet, if energised, caused the engine magnet to restore, stopping the horn, and this occurred when the distant signal was off. If the signal was at caution, the horn continued to sound and the brakes were gradually applied, but before this happened the driver would normally acknowledge the warning by operating a cancelling handle. It was a very simple system, and was being fitted by the LNER between Edinburgh and Glasgow when the war started, which equipment became the basis for the early BR experiments. To me it was a marvellous system which eased the strain of trying to see signals in bad conditions, and if distant signals were off, enabled the trains to run at full speed. The problem came when trains got close, and then distants were at caution, so that drivers were groping in the fog for the home signals, and delays mounted.

The approach to Fenchurch Street had been electrified by the LNER as part of the suburban electrification, and out through Stepney East to Bow it had its continuous colour light signalling, though without ATC. The GER and LNER had divided the suburban services between Fenchurch Street and Liverpool Street, but with electrification this had been concentrated onto Liverpool Street, and although the lines into Fenchurch Street from the GER had been electrified, only occasional special trains used them to keep the wires clean. Colour light signalling, with brightly lit signals at eye level are the answers to the driver's prayer, but they have one big snag; they are all the same, and it is all too easy to get lost! With old-fashioned signalling, each station has its distant, home and starter at least, and they are all different, so that they are individual, but colour light signals are all the same, each has its three or four aspects, so each one is like its successor. This was brought home forcibly to me one dark night driving out of Fenchurch Street. The main lines took a very sharp left turn at Stepney East, with a severe speed restriction through the junction and station. I suddenly found myself at Stepney East, when I thought I was one signal to go, and had to brake very hard. We went through the junction and station too fast for my comfort, and my mates made some caustic comments! Some days later, I heard that someone had shifted the track at Stepney East, a not uncommon occurrence.

On the other hand, continuous colour light signalling is marvellous when trains were following each other in quick succession. Coming down Brentwood Bank into Liverpool Street was the line which, in those days gave me that experience. On one occasion, I recall approaching such signals as they changed from double yellow to green. Then the signals were at double yellow, so we knew we were catching up the train in front, so eased off slightly and so were able to continue all the way, adjusting speed to match that of the train ahead.

I have already mentioned that the Tilbury Section was virtually self-contained, so far as its passenger workings were concerned. The LMS trains coming across North London from Kentish Town through Wood-grange Park stopped at Barking and did not even cross the LT District Line tracks. However, one exception was the boat trains operated chiefly in connection with Swedish Lloyd sailings to and from Tilbury. Sometimes they were worked by LMS 4Fs, but with the GER J17s replacing them on the LT&S, these engines started to work these trains over their circuitous route round North London through South Tottenham and Woodgrange Park to Kentish Town and St. Pancras. I went with one of them to experience the unusual route. The passengers got good value for their money in terms of ride, but I always wondered why, if Fenchurch Street wasn't considered a suitable station for a boat train, what was wrong with Liverpool Street, which already had continental boat trains, and would have been a much shorter and quicker journey?

The class 4 tanks were probably worked harder on the Tilbury section than anywhere else on a regular basis, and one of the most irritating failings with them was the refusal of the cylinder cocks to shut properly, due to bits of foreign matter, usually ash, getting under the mushroom valve. Most of the engines were fitted with self-cleaning smokeboxes, the idea of which is to eject only small ash through the chimney by making the gases sweep around the bottom of the smokebox by means of screens with deflector plates. Vertical mesh screens form the front part of the system, the idea being that larger pieces of ash would pulverise themselves against the mesh until small enough to pass through. This obviates the need to clean out the smokebox except at washouts, but one of the problems it caused was that to clean the tubes meant removing all the screens and putting

Inside the smokebox of a class 4 tank, with two mesh front screens removed, one in place, and deflector plates at front to help scour the front of the smokebox of ashes.

them back afterwards. Quite a lot of fine ash accumulated on top of the horizontal plate around the blast pipe, and of course when coasting with the regulator closed, some of it got sucked down the blast pipe and fell into the cylinder cocks. Sometimes, valve rings broke and these also found their way into the cylinder cocks. Lubrication, and excessive carbon build-up on the pistons and valves were all looked at, but no firm conclusions were ever reached.

As a result of delays with engines taking water at some of the water columns, it was decided that I should do some special tests. I was given 65552, a J17, for a day, and we went round from water column to water column, testing to see how long it took us to take water. Some columns gave very good flows, up to 1,000 gallons per minute, others were the reverse, and gave only a couple of hundred gallons or so in the same time. It did not matter in some cases whether it took five or ten minutes for shunting engines to fill their tanks, but at main line columns where engines needed to get water quickly, flow mattered. Of course, having taken 1,000 or 2,000 gallons of water at one column, we needed to get rid of it, so opened both injector water valves, and then every crew we passed would point to remind us we were losing water!

It was interesting to see that Upminster was the place with really good water supplies, around 750 gallons per minute, on the up and down main column, and one in the yard giving just 1,000 g.p.m. Tilbury station columns gave 400-500 g.p.m., the shed yard columns giving 800 g.p.m. Barking and Plaistow, and Southend and Shoeburyness columns gave very varying results, as low as 200 g.p.m. at one at Southend and 300 to 400 g.p.m. was quite normal. At Plaistow I was using Class 3 Tilbury tanks, with 1800 gallon capacity, and they were taking six and seven minutes to fill. Tank engines, with their smaller capacity and consumption, could manage with such flows, but for a main line tender engine needing quantities measured in thousands rather than hundreds, a good flow is essential or engines could be queuing up for water. At some depots this was a real problem at busy times, and often when several engines were taking water simultaneously the flows were drastically reduced. It was a problem at several depots.

I was then to spend nearly a year at Liverpool Street, firstly on the mechanical section and then with New Works. The Mechanical Section was led by E.H. "Teddy" Ker, whose assistants during my days at Liverpool Street included Colin Scutt, later to become C.M.E. of the Eastern Region, and Jack Somers, now retired to Wales, and one of the regular workers on the Festiniog Railway.

The new B.R. examination schedules, known as M.P.II, were being applied at Motive Power depots, and getting this organised and working properly was a job which many of us youngsters got involved with, both those working at depots, as well as at headquarters. Brakes, and failures due to ejectors being unable to create the proper 21" of vacuum, were also getting quite a lot of attention, and I visited most of the districts and principal depots analysing how the work was being done, and trying to get the standard procedures working regularly.

This was a period when the railways were recovering from the war and were starting to speed up services. In August 1952, tests were carried out on the Great Central main line on three days, 26th to 28th August, using 60056 with 300 tons, 350 tons and, finally, 400 tons. The timings were virtually the same for each day, in spite of the different loads, doing the journey from Aylesbury to Sheffield in 2 hours 20 minutes. I travelled with it on the third day, but have no particular memories of the journey.

A few days later, September 1st, I was with a similar special on the Great Northern line with *Mallard*, 60022, driven by her then regular driver, Joe Burgess, with Chief Inspector Sam Jenkins on the engine. A very fine ascent of Stoke bank came to an abrupt end when the middle big end failed at Corby Glen, but a few days later 60056 was showing her paces and did Doncaster to King's Cross in 142 minutes with a maximum of 90 at Little Bytham. 60056 had an unfortunate reputation at that time with injector failures and she had on several occasions failed completely from this cause until the problem was solved. The internal steam pipes were, I seem to recall, the cause of the problem.

On 17th November, it was the turn of the Liverpool Street to Southend line. It was to be investigated with an early morning non-stop run with a B1 and 10 coaches in 62 minutes down, 59 minutes up. On arrival at Southend, one third class coach was removed from the London end, and saloon 96 2451 was put on with Observation end leading. A number of the senior officers, including Leslie Parker himself, travelled down on the second trip, stopping at Shenfield and all stations onwards, and with two hours at Southend, there was plenty of time to partake of a good lunch in the saloon. It was seen that the engine crew were also provided with a good lunch, and liquid refreshment to wash it down, in the days when such pleasures and privileges were not abused.

Towards the end of the year I was transferred to the New Works Section, which was involved with the non locomotive side of the department, mess rooms, tools and equipment. Not very exciting tasks came our way, except when it meant a visit somewhere. To provide variation I periodically took an evening out to Shoeburyness with one of my Tilbury friends, or for a change, went out on the King's Cross suburban service. One of the Troop Sergeants in 157 Squadron (Supplementary Reserve), Fred Beckwith, was in the King's Cross "Met" link, with 9524 as his regular engine, and I continued to get practice in the art of quick stops with the vacuum brake for him. On the Great Northern suburban services going out to Hatfield or Hertford from Moorgate or Kings Cross with an N2, there was even less time to spare than on the Tilbury and as platform lengths had little to spare at many stations, so it was essential to stop in the right place first time, without too heavy a brake application. It took a lot of practice, as well as knowing the station and the engine and train sets, as the brakes and ejectors varied considerably. Another problem was that many of the stations are on a gradient, and at some of them, trains had to be held stationary with the brakes. As the engines had vacuum brake which could not be applied separately on the engine, as with steam braked engines, it was necessary to keep a little brake applied until the right away was given.

During the rush hour, the trains ran down into Moorgate over the "widened lines", and although the N2s were fitted with condensing gear, drivers very rarely used it. One night, I persuaded Fred Beckwith to condense to see how it worked, which we did, but when we got to King's Cross suburban, standing on the steep platform coming out of the "Hotel Curve", the flap valve, which closed the blast pipe and diverted the steam to the tanks, refused to open. We carried on up to Potters Bar, using the blower, and managed to keep steam and not lose much time, but by the summit the water in the tank was getting very hot and the injectors were playing up. Going through Hadley Wood Tunnels was like a good Turkish bath, the steam wasn't condensing and was exuding from the tanks everywhere. After going over the summit at Potters Bar, the level of the water in the boiler disappeared into the bottom nut of the gauge glass, so we more or less rolled down to Brookmans Park and Hatfield, making very gentle stops to avoid the water surging forward and uncovering the crown of the fire box and the lead plug. At Hatfield, we stopped right for the Water Column, and the fresh cold water enabled the injectors to work properly and refill the boiler, make up the fire and, eventually, go through to Welwyn Garden City after a slight delay.

In early 1953 I moved to King's Cross, and was working at Top Shed under Colin Morris, D.M.P.S., and John Simpson his assistant. The first job he gave me to do was to investigate the problems of the steaming of the A4s. All the 19 Eastern Region A4s were at that time at King's Cross, including three of the four of those fitted with double chimneys, 60022, 60033 and 60034. These three engines never gave trouble from lack of steam, and in fact many is the time when those engines would continue to work perfectly satisfactorily, though burning excessive amounts of coal, due to a defect like a leaking element joint. I still have a list of the delays due to engines being short of steam, totalling 505 minutes when working various of the more important trains, and a lot of time was spent investigating the more serious instances, often making special tests or examinations of the engines. It came back fundamentally to the problem that with good coal, carefully fired, the engines steamed adequately, but they had no reserve to cover the occasions when things were not one hundred per cent, which occured quite often in those days.

No. 60010, *Dominion of Canada* had been particularly troublesome, and when she was in for other repairs it was decided to do some tests, with a manometer fitted to indicate the smokebox vacuum. We first tried her as she was and put her on the 12.18 "Northumbrian" which was worked to Grantham and back. This was a no. 2 link job, and the driver for our first test was W. Hoole. We struggled up Stoke Bank, losing steam steadily, with only about 1½" water gauge of vacuum, going up to 2" when working very hard. The A4s had jumper tops to the blast pipe, a device whereby when the engine was working hard, the loose top of the blast pipe was supposed to lift, releasing the steam through annular slots and the larger orifice of the loose cap. We believed a lot of the problem was due to the jumpers not sitting back square, and so for the next test two days later, the jumper top had been fastened down solid. The transformation was remarkable, and the smokebox vacuum readings were very much more than before, from 2" to 3" under similar conditions, but the engine made steam and the fireman was able to maintain pressure right on the mark without difficulty. I had rarely ridden on A4s up until then, but felt able to have a go on the shovel on the return journey, starting an association with Bill Hoole which has very many happy memories.

Some experimental blast pipe tops were then made and tried. We were able to get even better results with an orifice in a flat plate to get the blast pipe orifice as low as possible, and with a larger diameter, but the advantages were minimal, and the simple expedient of fastening the jumper tops solid was sufficiently effective to get over the main problem. I did however fit the manometer onto 60033, one of the double chimney engines, and the readings were very much higher, 5" to 6", even more at times of very hard work and it was, of course, obvious why the double chimney engines with the Kylchap cowls steamed so freely.

I longed to pursue the experiments and would have liked to have tried a Kylchap cowl on a single chimney, something which I subsequently discovered had been tried on a pair of D49s way back in the late 1920s, but of which little record has survived.

One weakness of the three cylinder Gresley engines was a tendency for the right driving axlebox to run warm. When 60021 had a hot box, the opportunity was taken to fit a pair of thermometers into the crowns of the two driving boxes, and I rode with her to observe the performance. Unfortunately, I have not kept any records of the results, but I do particularly remember that when we stopped at Peterborough I was very worried to see the temperature go up considerably very quickly. When we got going, the temperature slowly dropped again.

The right hand box ran several degrees warmer than the left hand box, all the time. I tried standing the engine in the sun so that the left hand box would start warmer, but it did not take very many miles before the right hand became the warmer. The tests didn't prove anything, except to confirm that for some reason which has never been fully explained, the right hand box is slightly more heavily loaded and runs warmer, so that there is less margin for error once the white metal bearing starts to fail in any way, and a hot box results. Peter Townend recounts in his book how this was overcome by regular attention in the last years of steam.

The L1 tanks on the Marylebone service were a headache for the Neasden Shed Master, at that time, F.G. Clements, who recently retired as C.M.E. of B.R. The L1s were a very good engine for suburban work, powerful and with good acceleration, yet able to run quite fast when conditions allowed. However, they had design weaknesses which were never overcome, so that they were difficult engines to maintain, chiefly because they had insufficient bearing area in the axleboxes in proportion to their power, and consequently suffered hot boxes, as well as knocking themselves to pieces as the boxes got worn in the horns. Their other weakness was their slide bar bolts, which had a propensity to come loose or break, with disastrous results.

In those days it was the CME who told the Motive Power Department what engines should be used, to my mind the wrong way round. The object and purpose of a railway is to carry goods and people as economically as possible, for which it needs locomotives to haul the trains of a weight and at speeds as needed by the commercial requirements. The CME designs engines which he thinks will do the job, but if circumstances and conditions changed, it was a very difficult task to get the CME to modify a design to overcome faults. When I was trying to make *Dominion of Canada* steam, King's Cross and headquarters attempted to get permanent modifications, or double chimneys fitted to all the A4s, but the CME argued that the engines steamed satisfactorily and there was no justification for any change. It was only at the very end of steam that this attitude changed and the CMEs began to try to improve loco performance, but there was reluctance to spend money on steam engines which were about to be scrapped. Nevertheless, some long needed changes, such as double chimneys and improved middle big ends were done which cured the problems of the A4s (and A3s) so that they ended their days in a blaze of glory, substituting for failed diesels and working as intensively as them.

Every year I went to Longmoor with the Army Emergency Reserve for our annual camp, usually getting there a couple of days early in charge of the advance party. The unit grew each year, and our exercise on the Longmoor Military Railway in the second week became more interesting.

Woolmer in steam at Longmoor in 1954.

One year the exercise was made extra realistic with attacks on the stations and depots by infantry troops from other units. I was on the engine of a train which was attacked, as we were drawing into Longmoor Downs Station, with thunderflashes thrown onto the engine with the token. I told the driver to open up and get on away from it, instead of stopping. This was not quite what had been visualised, which rather upset the plans for the exercise, but what would most likely have been done in real wartime conditions, so no-one was quite sure what to say to me afterwards! One of the officers who joined us and took charge of one of the loco troops was Dick (R.H.N.) Hardy, then Shedmaster at Stewarts Lane, whose DMPS, Gordon Nicholson, was our O.C.

At camp in 1953, I got a message to go straight to King's Cross Station on the Monday morning after camp, prepared to go to Edinburgh on the first run of the summer time non-stop, which that year was renamed *The Elizabethan*. Three of us from Liverpool Street had the task of travelling in the front compartment used by the engine crews, and timing the train all the way. One of us hung out of the open window of the adjacent lobby trying to spot the quarter mileposts and stations, whereupon he thumped the coachside. The other two were reading the stop watch and plotting it on a graph. It was relatively easy to start with, as we all knew the route,

North of York, Inspector Jenkins waves as the down non-stop 'Elizabethan' overhauls a pair of Austerities. Taken from the Up 'Elizabethan' on 30th June 1953.

but as we got further north, we were on strange ground and many mileposts were hidden away from the lineside and are difficult to see from trains. In any case, going along the racing track north of York, we were doing the quarter miles in ten seconds, which didn't give us much time for reading stop watches, plotting the graph, etc. L.P. Parker himself, and several senior officers were with the train and periodically came to see how we were running against schedule and what speeds we were doing along the more interesting stretches. The Scottish crew had their lunch and went through to the engine, and the English crew – driver, Joe Howard – came back and washed and changed and went for their lunch. We were by that time getting hungry and thirsty, but could not leave our task, which had not been realised until Sam Jenkins, the Chief Inspector, discovered our predicament and went off to the Dining Car and got us some sandwiches and something to drink! However, we were all well fed and looked after that night in Edinburgh, and had a pleasant journey south next day, spending some of the time on the engine – 60028 *Walter K Whigham.*

In the autumn of 1953, Alan Pegler organised special trains to celebrate the Centenary of Doncaster Plant Works, which he called "The Plant Centenarian", and to work them he arranged for the two G.N. Atlantics, 990 and 251, to be extricated from the old Museum at York. 251 still had its superheated boiler, but in restoring her to the original appearance, the superheater header and elements had been removed. To make 251 steam reasonably it was necessary to fit restrictors into the flue tubes, and the two engines first ran a few trips from Doncaster through Lincoln to test them out.

They arrived at King's Cross from Doncaster on Friday 11 September, and were then stored, cleaned and generally prepared. I had suggested that drivers Hoole and Hailstone would make an excellent pair of drivers for the special, their turns of duty made them possible candidates, and I also thought it would be helpful if they could work a train together with the two engines, to get used to them. I arranged for them to work the 5.00pm ex King's Cross on two nights. This was normally a King's Cross B1 turn, which was first stop Hitchin, where the train split, the first portion going all stations main line to Peterborough, the rest to Cambridge. On the Wednesday night, I was at King's Cross Passenger Loco to see them off. When they appeared out of the tunnel King's Cross Signal Box 'phoned up Top Shed to enquire why there were two engines for the 5.00pm, and the expressions of the spotters at the end of the old no. 10 platform when these two stalwarts emerged from the tunnels down onto platform 6 was worth seeing. Alan Pegler's two confederates, Trevor Bailey and Les. Smith, had arranged to ride with Bill and Ted.

On the Thursday evening, I had quietly 'arranged' that I would join Bill Hoole, on 251, and Dick Hardy came over from Stewarts Lane to ride on 990 with his old friend, Ted Hailstone, who Dick had known well in the West Riding district. R.F. Harvey, chief of Motive Power, also came to see the engines leave, and as Dick had no official reason for being there,

Nos. 990 and 251 leaving Kings Cross on Wednesday 16th September 1953.

he had to make himself scarce, but he did manage to get into the front brake when the train left. Fortunately, after going through the tunnels we had signals 'on' at Holloway, so Ted, on 990 at the front, carefully over-braked, signalled to Dick, who jumped down onto the ballast, ran forward to 990, and joined them!

We had a good run down, which was not a particularly arduous task, but the return run was with a train of vans and coaching stock, and this gave us a little more work to do. The engines both went well and there were no problems for anyone, but it was fun firing an Atlantic, even if it was something of a hybrid. Unfortunately, I didn't see the actual specials, as I was on holiday.

CHAPTER VI

Breakdowns and visits

I have referred to joining the Supplementary Reserve (later the Army Emergency Reserve) when it was reformed in 1949. I was posted to 157 Loco Running Squadron, and in May 1949 I reported to Longmoor for the unit's first camp for about fifty civilians, ranging from chaps who had served right through the war and had become WOs, to young raw recruits. The O.C. was Major Sam Webster, Shed Master at Dover, and the second in command was Captain Henry Dannatt (who had been on the S.R. under Bulleid, but had recently left B.R. and was working as a civil servant) both of whom had several years war service. Having only just been demobbed, I possessed uniform, and had taken good care to come home from Germany well kitted out, which gave me a start, as the first few days were spent trying to sort out everyone to form the nucleus of a unit.

Whilst at camp that first year, the Longmoor Military Railway staff were making a film set of a rail crash for the film "Interrupted Journey", with Tom Walls and Valerie Hobson. Three of the old ambulance coaches were repainted into GWR colours on one side only, the end coach was lifted off its bogies at one end, the roof cut away, and an old Dean Goods engine, otherwise used for rerailing practice, lifted inside the coach, the whole being shunted by one of the big WDs. The second coach was lifted up with its buffers placed on a sleeper laid on the buffers of the first coach, and the third coach was used as a battering ram to make them telescope by being loose shunted down the siding, as fast as possible, by one of the WD tender engines. It was interesting to see the effect of the collision. The headstocks of the second and third vehicles gave way and the solebars splayed out, but things stuck for a while until the king pin of the middle coach sheared and allowed the body to ride through the first coach. Subsequently, I spent part of a night watching the actual filming – many of the locals, including troops from Longmoor and Bordon, had got jobs as extras – but as usual when the film was finished it formed only a few scenes in the story.

In October of that year, one of the big Eastern Region A1 Pacifics 60123 working a freight, ran into the back of a goods train on the Lincoln avoiding line. This line was worked under permissive block, in other words, proceed on sight, and it was a foggy night. The brake van of the train ended up at the bottom of the embankment, with the engine lying

Making the set for the film "Interrupted Journey" at Whitehill, May 1949.

nearly upside down on top of it, the front of the engine being just clear of the running lines.

Lincoln District had no cranes capable of lifting such an engine, and the Peterborough and Doncaster 45T cranes were allocated to do the job on a Sunday after some preparatory work had been done to anchor the front of the engine, and provide a platform on the embankment for the crane outrigger beams. Quite a gang of youngsters, like myself, as well as District Officers and Shed Masters, were present, and the first job was to drag the tender up the bank, lay it on its side at the top, roll it over and put

No. 60123 being hauled up the bank at Lincoln, 30th October 1949.

it on the track, a simple operation which only took just over an hour. The two cranes were then so positioned that they could both drag the back end of the engine up the embankment. Once that was on top of the bank, it was parallel with the track, and the cranes were repositioned so that the engine could be rolled over onto its wheels. It was then a simple rerailing job, which was completed just as it was getting dark.

For a job of this nature where the cranes are working to their limit,

Cranes rolling no.69552 onto its wheels at Edwinstowe on 10th September 1950.

planning and preparation are very essential. Apart from the anchor and foundations, the engine itself was prepared by removing the ashpan and firedoor, stripping the cab, and preparing an attachment through the firehole door to which the two cranes could fasten to haul it up the bank.

The following weekend, the Grimsby Crane came to pick up the brake van and the remaining bits and pieces.

A year later an N2 hauling a Mansfield – Edwinstowe train derailed and ended up on its side at the bottom of a bank, lying away from the line. Colwick and Doncaster cranes did this job, and it was even more tricky than the A1 because of the distance the engine was lying away from where the cranes stood. In this case, an anchor had been made to fit on top of the dome, and the cranes were absolutely at their limit when rolling the engine up onto its wheels and starting to lift it up the bank. As the engine started to come up the bank, the radius of the cranes reduced, the lift became more vertical, and the problem was over, but before this the back wheels of the cranes were lifting from the rails, and the dog clips which are used to anchor the cranes to the track were lifting it up from the ballast. Although heavy foundations had been put down for the cranes, dug into the side of the embankment, these naturally consolidated under the pressure, and the cranes had to be well bedded down before they took the full load.

After the engine was lifted up, there were the carriages, but they were relatively straightforward.

Two months after this, an Austerity rolled down the bank at Ulceby, again ending upside down. The Grimsby and Doncaster cranes were used and again lifted the tender first, then the engine, upside down onto the formation, and then rolled them over and put them back onto the track. In this case, the bank was not so high, and the engine was not so far from

No. 79242 (90690) slung between two cranes at Ulceby, 12th November 1950.

The load gauge and mirrors behind the 04s at Immingham, 7th March 1953.

the track, and from a 7.30 start, the engine was back on its wheels by 11.00.

In all these cases I took a series of photographs at various stages of the job; 60123 being near Lincoln town, and readily accessible, was extensively photographed by several people, but few saw the other incidents.

Another exercise in which Father was involved was the righting of the *SS Hebble* in Immingham Docks. In the East Coast floods at the end of January 1953, the sea had flooded the dry dock in which the *Hebble* was lying, and she capsized. When the floods subsided and the water was pumped out, preparations were made for righting the vessel, by sealing off the deck openings and mounting 'A' frames on the side of the hull, connected to various capstans. The Motive Power involvement was to provide additional help in the form of a pair of 04s coupled to a long rope through a pulley system. It was very important that the various haulages were co-ordinated so that the loadings were equalised or disaster could have occurred, so the engines (double heading) were coupled to a spring balance set up on a trolley, with a framework above carrying a mirror so that the drivers could read the load being applied. "Walkie talkies" were

SS Hebble *in the dock at Immingham on 7th March 1953.*

in use so that the Controller could co-ordinate the effort, and as water was let in to the dock, so the capstans and the 04s were to haul away, so that as *Hebble* floated again, she righted herself. She was then overhauled and sailed the seas for several years more. *The Empress of Canada* turned over similarly in Liverpool's Gladstone Dock due to water used on a fire on board, and Liverpool Dock officials came to watch the *Hebble* operation. With miles of wire ropes running everywhere, there was a real danger of lashing ropes if anything had gone wrong, but it was an interesting operation to see, even from a distance. It was Father's birthday, but his assistant, Harold Darley, as well as his two Lincoln Inspectors, Cummings and Timms, accompanied us, and we all had a day which they often referred to as "Hebble Day".

Most of the Railway Works had societies for the apprentices, which arranged meetings and visits to works of railway interest, for which the Railway gave travel and other facilities. During my time at Doncaster, I

Inside Crewe works on 12th August 1949.

went to Crewe, Gorton, Cowlairs and Swindon, as well as LTE Acton and Yorkshire Engine Company, then building WR Pannier Tanks. At some works, such as Crewe, we were shown round by the ordinary guides, but at other places technical staff showed us around, and this made it much more interesting. I particularly recall Acton where things were very different from that to which we were accustomed. We were taken into a driving cab, with the motors isolated, and were then allowed to operate the controls and watch the contactors notching round, etc. Swindon had

its optical methods of lining up frames and horns, rather more sophisti-
cated than the wire we were accustomed to using, and somehow Swindon
had that aura of a Works where they had really got to grips with the
problems of giving steam locos thorough overhauls so that they were
returned to service in a condition as nearly as good as new as was possible.
We certainly got the feeling at Crewe that there was a great effort to turn
the engines out as quickly as possible, an attitude which nationalisation
was bringing to Doncaster in the form of Heavy Intermediate Repairs.
Under BR, the repair of engines was controlled by the Shopping Bureau,
who seemed to exist primarily to provide the main Works with a con-

Milan, 26th May 1950.

Italian outside valved, inside cylinder 2–6–0.

tinuous programme of work. It is said that railways are run for the con-
venience of railwaymen rather than for the benefit of the customers, and
there is some truth in the remark. I often felt that railway organisations
sometimes overlooked the object of the railway – to serve the customer –
though I feel that politicians have rather endorsed that attitude.

In LNER days, depots or sheds programmed the visits of their
locomotives to main Works so that they had the maximum numbers of the
right type of loco at the right time. For example, the passenger engines
were all wanted in the summer, whereas the heavy freight engines were
needed in the winter for coal traffic, so it was arranged that so far as
possible the freight engines went through main works in the summer and
the passenger engines in the winter. Similarly, K3s and mixed traffic
engines were wanted in East Anglia for the soft fruit in the spring. Sheds
used to plan for this by analysing the condition of the engines, nursing

GW push-pull train at Birmingham, Snow Hill.

those in better condition to make them last to the end of the busy season, whilst the engines in worst condition would be used to the maximum and got to main works and back ready for the busy season. After Shopping Bureaus came into being, engines were only accepted into works when they had worked up the appropriate mileage, unless the depot could prove that there was a definite serious defect. This meant that sometimes there were serious shortages of appropriate types of engines to shift heavy traffic, which was highlighted one summer when Doncaster had an inordinate number of Pacifics in shops over August Bank Holiday weekend, causing quite a shortage of big engines to work the heavy holiday traffic, necessitating the use of V2s and B1s with all the problems of overloading, lost time, etc. As a result of this, main works were requested to minimise the number of big passenger engines held under repairs over holiday periods.

A very old friend of the family spent the War with Movement Control, the section of the Royal Engineers which programmed the movement of personnel and stores on railways, ships and any other available form of transport. He was in Hamburg whilst I was in Germany, and I had a couple of visits to him there, and then he was in Trieste whilst I was at Doncaster. This gave me an excuse to go out to stay with him – in those days, holidays abroad were tricky to arrange with currency restrictions then in force. It involved a long journey across Europe by steam and electric traction from Calais through Paris and Vallorbe to Milan. Several things stand out in my memory of the journey, such as Domodossola, where the Italian and Swiss imcompatible overhead electrification met, where the train coasted into the station with pantograph down, the electric loco then being shunted by a steam loco back to the departure end of the station. The sight of an Italian Pacific under the overall roof of Milan station, belching out black smoke, with a tender neatly piled high with coal bricquettes, was a sight which would never have been allowed in Britain, and contributed to the carriage door handles being the dirtiest I had ever handled! The Italians had some inside cylinder 2–6–0s, but with the piston valves outside, operated with Walschaerts valve gear, including a dummy connecting rod! It looked even more odd than old 'Tishy', LMS 25845, that used to work occasionally from Bletchley to Cambridge.

The Italians, like the Germans, still used four wheeled coaches for suburban and local services, some of them of quite modern design.

At Trieste, part of the tramway system to Oppacine had a very steep gradient with rope worked bankers pushing the tram up the hill, sometimes with a bicycle on the front! At Paris, the suburban services were worked by 2–8–2 tank engines operating in push-pull, which ran into the terminus just like an electric train, and then left with the steam engine pushing a large number of coaches from behind. This was a novel experience, something which British railways were subsequently to prove was perfectly safe, but for more modern propulsion. In steam days, it was not permissible to propel more than two coaches in Britain, except in special circumstances, hence the SR & GWR push-pull practice of an engine sandwiched between two pairs of coaches. It was only with the advent of the Bournemouth electrification that tests were done to verify flange forces when propelling, and thus permit propulsion of larger trains at main line speeds.

CHAPTER VII

A permanent appointment – ATC Assistant

When I got back to King's Cross after my holiday at the end of September 1953, I was told that I had been appointed to a new position at Liverpool Street under Leslie Parker, Motive Power Superintendent, as Assistant responsible for ATC, as it was then called, (it is known as AWS today). Looking back, I wonder very much how the great Leslie Parker had arranged my training with this move in view, since my spell at Plaistow gave me experience with the "Hudd" system and then I had been at King's Cross when the BR system was first introduced. I did not even have an interview for the job, and it involved me jumping a grade but L.P. Parker told Father that it put me on a par with colleagues of my age who hadn't had to spend time in the Forces. It meant that I was graded Special 'A', which entitled me to First Class travel, and also gave me a footplate pass for the Eastern Motive Power Area, endorsed that I was authorised to instruct enginemen in their work.

At the same time that I got the letter telling me of the new appointment, I also received a note, though written a week earlier, telling me that LPP wanted me to undertake some tests with certain Britannias which were reported to slip very badly when running at speed, 70039 being the worst offender. This particular batch of engines had been built with roller bearings on the driving axle, but plain bearing boxes on leading and trailing coupled axles. On the last batches of Britannias roller bearings and plain boxes for the driving axles were tried, in various combinations.

Stratford had looked at 70039 very closely, checking the weights on the various axles as well as the wheel and tyre diameters. All proved reasonable for an engine which had run 59,000 miles. The regulator (multiple valve type) was also checked. No problems seemed to occur up to about 55 mph, and in the hands of its regular drivers, there were no problems, with timekeeping maintained.

When the apparent slipping occurred, it was sometimes difficult to stop it, even after shutting the regulator, and it was necessary to use the steam brake. Whilst it was thought that this may have been due to the regulator not closing properly, this did not explain the slipping in the first place. Like everyone else, I was completely baffled, and to try to prove what was happening, it was arranged to fit a speedometer to the engine, and this showed that when the acute vibration occurred, there was no significant change in the wheel speed; in other words, the driving wheels were not actually slipping, but after one of the trips one of the side rod bushes were running warm and it was found that the side rod was slightly bent, another sign, normally, of the effects of slipping! It was then decided to drop the wheels out, when it was found that the cause of the trouble was that the axleboxes were seizing in the horns. Of course with a pair of wheels not properly running on the rails, it would give excessive vibration on the engine!

When I was at Doncaster, the last batch of A1 Pacifics had been fitted with roller bearings, partly as an experiment for the Britannias, and they had had similar problems. I remember seeing some of the axleboxes and horn cheek liners when removed, and they looked like a ploughed field. I was astounded that a component that has relatively small movement, could seize up so that the metal was picking up and tearing in such a manner. It seemed that the problem with the Britannias persisted for many years, as Bill Harvey quotes cases some five years later, where it was still happening.

The drawings showed a clearance of .008" for the axleboxes in the horn cheeks, but in practice it was found necessary to give about .025" clearance when new, and then when the manganese liners had work hardened, and bedded in, they could be shimmed up to give about .015" clearance. This clearance would then remain for the life of the engine until the next visit to shops. Another case of the running sheds having a cure for a problem not fully appreciated by the Works.

When I was appointed to the new job, it was hoped that approval would be given before long for an extension of the system of ATC, but it was still suffering from teething problems, though many of these could be traced to the experimental nature of the equipment. Above all, part of my job was to try to give drivers confidence in the ATC equipment, so that they would appreciate its value. With men who had not been brought up with ATC, there was a lot of conservatism towards its adoption, and a feeling that they had managed without it for the best part of their lives, and couldn't really see the value of it. Admittedly, from a footplateman's standpoint, colour light signalling, or electrically lit semaphores were a good answer, and saved the strains and worries of spotting signals, particularly at certain locations, but ATC also gave that additional safeguard that if a driver misread a distant signal, he was given an audible warning and a physical stop if he did not heed it. The GWR had had their system working for many years, which had given that railway an enviable safety record, but it was a system which relied on physical contact of a shoe under the engine with a ramp in the track, and it was alleged that the system had limitations at high speeds, had problems on electrified lines and was prone to wear. The Hudd System on the LT & S, as referred to in my earlier chapter relied on magnetic induction between track and receiver, on loco or driving cab, the permanent magnet giving the warning, and the electro magnet, energised if the signal was off, providing a restoring action, so that the system was fail safe. The LNER was putting in a Hudd system after the Castlecary disaster between Glasgow and Edinburgh in December 1937, but the outbreak of war stopped it, and the equipment went into store.

When BR was formed, one of the safety measures that it agreed should be implemented was the development of a universally acceptable ATC system, and a development section was set up especially for the purpose. They resuscitated the LNER Hudd equipment from Scotland, but instead of the armature in the receiver opening a small valve and the system being worked by the vacuum, it was decreed by the Railway Inspectorate that a separate and distinctive audible warning was necessary for the clear indication. This involved fitting the engine with electric batteries – Nife Accumulators – and the armature then operated electrical contacts. Electrical equipment does not take kindly to the dirt and vibra-tion of the steam locomotive, and it took a long time for the S & T boffins to design and produce equipment which would work, and continue to work reliably, in the way safety signalling equipment is required to work. In October 1953, the Harrow and Wealdstone disaster put the public spotlight onto ATC, and from a development which was quietly pro-ceeding in a few back rooms, it became an experiment of considerable importance.

I felt then, and do so equally today, that far too much money is spent by many organisations in complicating and elaborating equipment which inevitably gives more cause for failure. In transport that inevitably means less reliability. The GWR had a good, reliable ATC system, which was well proven. The LT & S had the Hudd, which was equally well proven, though admittedly on a much smaller scale, but was a very simple system – and avoided electrics. The Hudd could have been extended throughout BR at a fraction of the cost of the development and fitting up of the BR system, and, if it had been adopted could have become universal on the main lines years earlier than in fact happened, and would probably have saved several of the more notable accidents of recent years. But for the war, the LNER would undoubtedly have developed and extended it considerably. Unfortunately, the Railway Inspectorate insisted on differ-ing indications for clear and warning signal aspects, but they do not have responsibility for BRs finances. What price safety?

All somewhat akin to the rush into dieselisation, which, it is generally agreed, was done with indecent haste and waste. I realise the limitations of steam, and that it is not compatible with modern needs, but I believe that railways should be electrified, and there should have been, and should still be, an ongoing electrification programme, as happened in Europe. With the modern fleet of steam locos BR had, and improve-ments that were made in the last years, they could have been kept going properly and phased out as electrification took over, with diesels and DMUs for the lightly trafficked lines and areas. The Newcastle suburban electrification has come back again, albeit in a modern form, and I believe that unless there is a radical development in energy storage, more power will have to be provided by electricity generated from natural resources, hydro power, winds, tides, etc., and as transport by rail is the one form of transport that can readily use electricity, electrified railways will become very necessary as the prime means of transport. Oil (and coal) are not being created, and geologically speaking, there are only very finite resources of them. They are capital resources, and, once used up, there will be no more. If anyone tries to live on capital, bankruptcy eventually occurs. We must learn to live on energy sources which will always be available and will last virtually forever. I digress, nevertheless railways have their backs to the wall financially; a railway accident is rare and news. Safety is paramount on railways, the public expect it, but are not prepared to pay for it, and I feel that if we are not careful we shall end up with almost absolutely safe railways that no one can afford to use.

In 1953, there were 54 engines fitted with the ATC, 11 A1s, 7 A3s, 19 A4s, 12 V2s and 5 WD Austerities. The signals equipped were on the down main from New Barnet to Huntingdon, with mostly semaphore signalling. This means the distants – so that the practical usage of the equipment only occurred with main line trains from King's Cross. The 19 A4s were all at King's Cross, and virtually every time they went out, they went over the test section, and they gave the bulk of the practical experience, but the A1s at Leeds, and A3s at Grantham worked into King's Cross irregularly, turn and turn about with non fitted engines, while the V2s and WDs often went on the slow line and it was possible thereby to bypass all the signals equipped with track magnets.

The technicalities of the equipment were under the control of the ATC development section led by Mr. J.H. Currey (a signal engineer and a clever boffin), who was situated at Marylebone. At King's Cross a specialist maintenance team had been built up under the leading brake fitter. Although the sheds responsibilities were only to record malfunctions and change units when they failed, as King's Cross engines provided the bulk of the operating experience, the experience of the King's Cross ATC staff in diagnosing what part of the equipment was faulty, and helping to keep it fully operative, was invaluable. At other sheds the ATC equipment was just another job, and although they looked after it, they did not get the same amount of work and experience. My task was to provide liaison between the sheds and Mr. Currey and his staff, to follow up failures and, particularly, to fly the ATC flag to enginemen. The top link King's Cross men, with their regular A4s became very enthusiastic about ATC, just like the Tilbury men, and as the equipment became more reliable, got very cross if the equipment on their regular engine wasn't working. With continued development and changes, there weren't enough spare sets and at times if a unit failed there wasn't another to replace it. However, as enthusiasm for the equipment grew, I emphasised to Marylebone the importance of keeping the A4s working, so that confidence in it was maintained, and as production equipment became more universal, rather than the old Hudd equipment adapted for experimental purposes, so reliability improved.

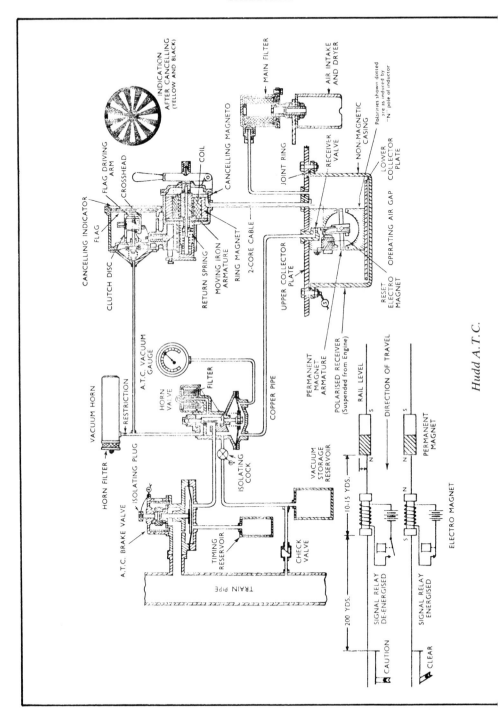

Hudd A.T.C.

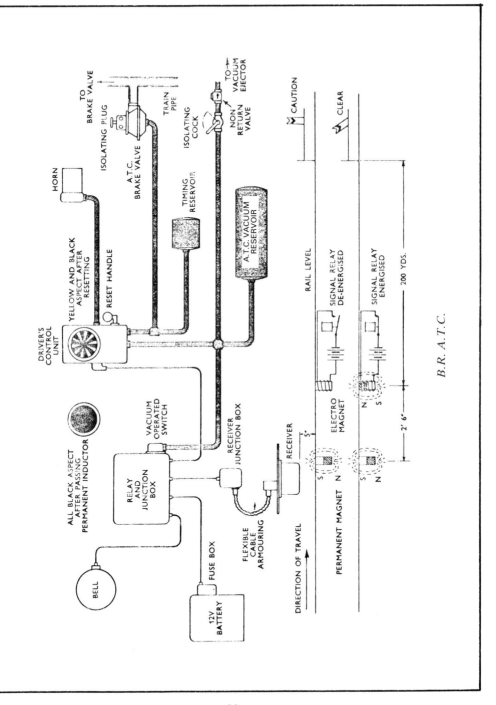

B.R. A.T.C.

Investigating faults was routine, but the continual development and changes of equipment involved not only riding on the engines to see how things worked in service, but visiting the four sheds having the engines to tell them what was coming. I also went to other sheds where drivers worked to King's Cross, arranging for an ATC fitted engine (in working order!) to be there in steam, and then demonstrated to drivers and inspectors how it functioned and how to work it. A large hand magnet passed under the engine receiver at the front of the engine, with the appropriate pole uppermost, enabled the bell and horn to function and for the brake application to be observed, as well as the effect of cancelling a warning indication.

One fundamental change was made to the driver's control equipment quite early on. The original equipment had mechanical operation of the rotating indicator, so that when a caution signal was cancelled, the indicator went to alternate yellow and black segments, but, being mechanical, the indicator could be put to this position by depressing the handle. It was restored to black by the next permanent magnet. The developed equipment did both operations electrically, and contacts were arranged so that the indicator would only go to alternate yellow/black if the receiver actually had received a warning indication. When the receiver was in the normal position, depressing the driver's handle had no effect on the flag.

The driver's control unit is the link between the electrical system and the brakes, and primarily consists of a solenoid, which operates a small disc valve. This solenoid is normally held up by being energised by current from the accumulators via the normal contacts of the receiver. When this current fails, either from the receiver being operated or any other reason, the solenoid falls and ports in the disc valve open, admitting air into the timing reservoir and brake valve, applying the brakes gradually. Another port connects the ATC horn to the main ATC vacuum reservoir, sounding the horn.

The solenoid is not self-restoring, i.e. it will not lift itself up by the electricity being restored, so it has to be restored by depressing the handle on the side of the driver's unit. This action also restores the receiver, by means of energising a small coil in it, as well as operating the driver's indicator.

An electrical condenser is connected across the solenoid, so that it does not drop immediately the circuit is broken by the receiver contacts. This is so that when the receiver is operated and then restored by the track electro magnet energised because the signal is at clear, the solenoid does not drop and give a warning indication, but electrical contacts are arranged so that the bell sounds.

Messrs Plessey, whose works were behind the electric depot at Ilford, were interested in the development, and produced a special relay unit of their own which we tried on 60003. *Andrew K. McCosh*. It was very special in that it had no moving parts, and worked perfectly well. At the time it was shrouded in secrecy and mystery to us, but was obviously an early application of solid state circuitry.

It was a very interesting job, and was quite hectic to start with as the various changes in the equipment were in progress, and with the tremendous interest in ATC, I was giving talks on it both to railway people and others at many places. It gave me a lot of travelling around, most of which was on the footplate, with plenty of opportunity to travel with some of the many friends I had gained. By the time I was leaving BR, adoption and extension was nigh, and the work had become much more routine.

CHAPTER VIII

Footplate memories

When I moved to Liverpool Street in 1951, I got a footplate pass for the Eastern Motive Power Area, and was able to get home to Lincoln virtually every weekend. On Sunday evenings there was a service to Spalding, which connected with the Cleethorpes – King's Cross train. This had an Immingham B1, and with twelve well-loaded coaches, was a pretty tough assignment. Immingham was the biggest shed in the Lincoln district, the only one with main line workings, of which the Cleethorpes–London train was its most difficult.

Various workings had been tried for this train, and one suggestion made to try to improve them was to make it a lodging job for Grimsby men, but they were not prepared to lodge, so the little shed at Boston offered to take it. Boston was a small country depot which worked local trains to Peterborough, Grimsby, Grantham, Lincoln, etc., but the Chairman of its Local Departmental Committee, Sam Brockett, was very keen to get more work for the depot, and had been at King's Cross. Father arranged a volunteer link of six crews to Boston to work the Cleethorpes train from Boston to London, and from Grimsby, where the train reversed, to Boston. Additionally, they worked the Grimsby fish train from Boston to King's Cross, another tough assignment with K3s. This gave keen and experienced regular crews, but it also required first rate B1s in top condition, and Father, his Shed Masters at Immingham, and George Emmerson, his Chief Inspector, all spent a lot of time trying to improve the workings to avoid delays. Two other Immingham workings required good B1s, namely the Birmingham and Manchester trains, but they were not as tough as the up London trains, and, most particularly, the Sunday night train. During the middle of the week, the London train normally had nine coaches, with eleven coaches on Monday, Friday and Sunday, but the up train on Sunday evening, which did not have a balancing working, the engine taking fish empties back north, was twelve coaches always fairly full, and was the toughest of the lot. The problem with the up working was that the hardest part of the run, from Peterborough to London, non-stop, came at the end of the run, when the fire had been going for several hours and was, therefore, beginning to develop clinker unless the coal was of good quality. The long runs used far more coal than on most of the workings normally done by the engines, and consequently, unless special arrangements were made, only a limited amount of the grade one coal, which Immingham had for the three long runs, also for the K3s on the fish trains, could be loaded onto the tender, and by the time Peterborough was reached this would all be used up and all that which was in the bottom of the tender would be a selection of nutty slack which had accumulated over quite a long time. When the engine got to King's Cross, it was able to coal up with enough for the complete run and in any case in the down direction, the hardest part from King's Cross to Peterborough was when the fire was fresh and the best coal on the front of the tender. This coal problem was overcome by ensuring that the workings of engines used on these longer runs were carefully programmed beforehand, so that the coal in the tender was used up as far as possible. This remaining coal should then have been brought forward before loading up with the grade one coal, so that the maximum amount of it possible was put on the tender and not just a small amount at the front.

Eventually, Immingham had a routine that the London engine would be washed out on Saturday, after running the tender low on Friday, then working the Sunday evening train, and the daytime trains until the following Sunday. Many were the struggles we had on Sunday nights to get through without losing time. It was a busy time of the evening, and if that train ran late, it delayed others. Not only was the coal and fire a problem, but other things could go wrong as well, such as rows of brick arch falling down in the fire, until Immingham shed really made sure that the London engine was turned out in first-class condition. Only the best B1s were used for London workings, and every B1 as it came out of the Works after repairs was ridden by Inspector Emmerson and passed as fit for working to London. Normally, when the engines became due for valve and piston exams, they came out of the London list, and several engines never went on it. *Mayflower* (No. 61379) was the worst engine of the bunch, she was never any good and even though Doncaster Works went through her with a fine tooth comb, they found nothing to account for the poor performance. However, in view of the association of her name with Boston, she was used on the mid-week trains with the lighter loads, but only rarely on Sunday nights. Whilst I enjoy driving suburban trains where there is satisfaction in stopping neatly in the right spot in the platform with the brakes nearly off, ready for a quick start, main line driving on the B1s did not have the same appeal, particularly as it was usually necessary to keep such a close watch on the boiler. The stop at Peterborough, which had to be right for taking water, demanded a lot of confidence. Sam Brockett and Syd Tutty trusted me to do it and I never let them down, but as I gained experience, I got far more satisfaction from firing than ever I got from driving on expresses.

When I was at Liverpool Street, it was common for we young men to arrange jobs away on Mondays or Fridays. Occasionally, I managed to have some small investigation at Lincoln or Boston to do on a Monday morning, so that I could go up on the Cleethorpes from Boston, and, if possible, I arranged things so that George Emmerson would also be there. It was really good to have opportunities to work under my old

No. 61379 with driver Luffman passing Offord on the 4pm Kings Cross – Cleethorpes.

tutor, and by the time I moved to King's Cross in 1953, I was usually taking the shovel. Sometimes it was possible to arrange an evening out with my Boston friends, particularly on the week when Syd Tutty was on the 4.00 pm down Cleethorpes and Sam Brockett on the Up Fish. It gave me time to have a quick bite at Boston – sometimes Syd took me to his home for a meal – and Sam would tell his fireman to keep the Guard company, as K3s weren't the most comfortable engines to ride on as spare man. There is nothing like having the job to do alone, to gain confidence! Sam was not unlike Bill Hoole, he believed in getting a move on, and he would let the signalman know that he wanted a good run. He really rattled the K3s on the Fish so as to keep ahead of the expresses and stay on the main line as far south as possible before getting put onto the slow line.

Grimsby men were very cross seeing Boston men gaining main line work, with its extra money for mileage, and tried very hard to get the work back, but Father told them that they had their chance and refused it, and he thoroughly supported Boston. Similarly, some of the older men at

Boston thought that they should be in the London link, but Father refused to alter the existing arrangements. Sam used to lobby me in his support for Father against such pressures; they both said that the existing volunteers would remain in the link so long as they wished, but replacements would be selected as the LDC wanted.

Sam Brockett was also on the Local Town Council, and sometimes I fear his mind was not properly on the job, so that he had an unfortunate record of passing signals at danger. Father fought hard for him, but told him that he could not go on doing so. Not long after Father retired, Sam ran past signals with the fish empties coming out of King's Cross Goods, and put his engine on the floor, which was the end of Sam's driving, and, sad to relate, he died not long afterwards. There was a story that in his firing days at King's Cross Sam, on one occasion, actually shovelled so much coal on the fire of a Met N2 that he put it out!

One of his epic runs was with 1408 on Sunday 26th July 1953, when the train was made to 13 coaches, about 389 tons, yet we passed Hitchin two minutes early and got into King's Cross six minutes ahead of time. Of course, there was recovery time in the schedule anyway, but the B1s, even with twelve on, would not normally make up much time. 1408 was one of the best of the bunch, and she was a very regular London engine, along with 1079, 1098, 1130, 1142, 1144 and 1175, but it was the 1300s that were shy, and 1379 the worst of all!

The condition of the B1s turned out by Immingham for the London, steadily improved, particularly when John Peck became Shed Master (now retired from BR Leeds, but involved with inspecting the engines at Barry in conjunction with the National Railway Museum). In the mid-50s, Lincolnshire was the second area to be turned over to DMUs, and George Emmerson was becoming increasingly busy with training drivers and therefore unable to give the same attention to the London engines as previously, so he and John Peck used me as an unofficial extra Inspector for the London B1s! John Peck would check with Father to see if I was coming home at a weekend, and would then put an engine on the Sunday evening for me to try out, on which I would then report back to Father on Monday morning, who would let John Peck know. Although we rarely met, a friendly relationship built up between us.

Although I say it myself, if I could not make a B1 steam, few else could, and one of the nicest compliments I had was from a Stratford driver. Mother and Father were staying at Mundesley, Norfolk, and I had gone there to join them for the weekend. On the Sunday evening I was returning on a special from Norwich, which was very full, so I went up to the engine, showed my pass, and joined them. The engine was 1372, one of *Mayflower*'s cousins, so I wasn't expecting anything very exciting, but when I saw the way the fireman was working, I wondered what would happen, as he just filled the firebox up as we climbed out of Norwich, and then sat down. 1372 didn't like it, but once through Tivetshall it is easy going, particularly going down through Haughley. It was obvious though that the rest of the run wouldn't be easy, and talking to the driver at

Ipswich, he was quite prepared to let me have a go on the fire. I set to with the pricker to try to push down the mountain in the centre of the firebox, as it is quite impossible on a B1 to do anything with a fire like that, and as we left that station, closed the trap to make it burn through. The trap is the small flap door within the big door, through which the firing is done. It is hinged horizontally and normally is left open to give secondary air above the fire, to aid combustion and reduce smoke. Though the actual flap is like a butterfly valve, there is solid plate above the hinge and a ratchet on the top half to keep it open, or vary its opening if desired. The GE lines had been laid as cheaply as possible and followed the contour of the land so that although East Anglia has few hills of much importance, the profile of the lines tend to be like a saw, and Ipswich to London has most of the principal stations in river valleys, with climbs over the ridges between. By the time we got to Colchester, I had got the fire as I wanted, and I was firing in my usual way of twice round the box as each lot got burnt through. No. 1372 was steaming quite well and as we went up the final rise from Chelmsford through Ingatestone and Shenfield to Ingrave summit, I felt very pleased. Driver Copelap was also very pleased with what I had done, and wanted to know where I was from as he would liked to have had me with him regularly! The train was stopping at Ilford, and I was getting off there, and he was most surprised when I told him I was at Head Office and how I had learnt to fire B1s, but it was a very nice compliment to me!

I had gained experience on the A1s going home on the 6.18pm, but with them no great skill was needed, just an ability to put enough coal on to do the job. It wasn't until I got to King's Cross in 1953 that I had opportunities to get onto A4s, and the experiments with 60010s blast pipe with Bill Hoole and later with others initiated me into the firing of the Gresley engines, as distinct from just shovelling in coal as on the A1s.

When I was involved with the 'slipping' Britannias, I sometimes fired them, but found it far more tiring to fire a Britannia for the 115 miles from London to Norwich, than an A1 or A4 to Grantham (105 miles) or beyond. I found the LMS type sliding doors and large firehole much hotter and more difficult with which to manipulate the shovel to direct the coal so that it would go where wanted. Probably it was because I wasn't accustomed to it. On the other hand, LMS men found the small opening of an Eastern flap door quite difficult to fire through; they weren't used to having to have the coal small to get through such a small opening, and of course they found that they hit the door with the shovel and spilt coal on the floor. I wouldn't have liked to fire a Britannia all the way to Leeds, yet I would happily fire an A4 or A1 down to Leeds in the morning and another one back in the afternoon or evening.

At the end of steam, Alan Pegler several times invited Dick Hardy and/or myself on to some of the specials being worked by his *Flying Scotsman* when she was working over Shap or Ais Gil. I particularly remember one occasion when he had come over from Leeds to Manchester. I joined the engine going from Manchester to Preston, where I went into

The author in the drivers seat of Sir Nigel Gresley, *with his hand on the reverser.*

the tender to help pull coal forward. I went back on the engine as the train started, to find the fireman with the big door open firing away, not just putting big lumps in the back corners, as I would probably have done. She did a little slip as we started, whereupon the flame scoop slid down, stopping further firing, so I took the shovel from the fireman, using it to lift the scoop back into place, shut the big door and opened the 'trap' – the small door within the main door with which most LNER engines were fitted – whereupon the fireman commented, "You can't fire through that little

97

hole." I proceeded to show him how it was done and he then took the spare shovel and we took it in turns to give her a round. By the time we got to Carlisle he had widened his experience and mastered the technique, but it illustrated the difference in firing techniques for different engines.

Soon after I was appointed to the ATC job, all inspectors and supervisors riding on engines were asked to report on delays observed when travelling with important trains, and I started keeping logs of many of my runs, which I still have. I have always believed that a railway has an obligation to its passengers to get them to their destination safely and comfortably, when the timetable plans that they should arrive. I believe that punctuality and reliability, so that connections and appointments can be made readily, is as, if not more, important that clipping the odd minutes off schedules. The passenger is not very bothered about why the train is late, he only knows that it is late and he is being inconvenienced. Some drivers were against trying to regain lost time, and would blame every minute from PW checks, signals, etc., to explain their late arrival, and argued that they did not see why their fireman should be made to work harder because of delays from causes which were not their fault. Of course, other drivers took the opposite view, particularly those like Bill Hoole, who never carried a watch, and seemed to have one aim – to get there as quickly as possible! I enjoyed firing to Bill, or to anyone else who would try to get the train to its destination on time. I used to say that if I was firing, I didn't mind how hard I worked, and I have told several drivers to open the regulator a bit more and try to get the train through on time. Nevertheless, I didn't like Bill's way of running early and then getting checked by signals.

I got on well with virtually all the King's Cross and Copley Hill (Leeds) top link drivers, though naturally I had my particular friends. I kept the King's Cross and Copley Hill rosters in my log book in my case with my overalls, etc., with the driver's names, written in order, twice, on a separate piece of paper; as they moved one job each week, I only had to move my list of names down one to see where everyone was. The main London workings of Copley Hill men were as follows:

Dia 11　　: Work 10.45 Leeds to KX &3.50 to Leeds.
Dia 31/2 : Work 4.35 Leeds to KX, Queen of Scots, lodge in London and work down 7.50 KX–Leeds.
Dia 33/4 : Work 6.26 Leeds; KX, lodge in London and work down 12.05 KX–Leeds, Queen of Scots.

The 7.50 am ex-King's Cross, at around that time, was the fastest train in the country, Hitchin to Retford, splitting at Doncaster into four coaches for Leeds, the remaining six coaches going to Newcastle, the 6.26 pm ex-Leeds being the corresponding up working. The engine and crew that worked the up Queen of Scots lodged in London and worked the down 7.50 am "flyer" the next day, whereas the engine and crew working the up "flyer" 6.26 pm ex-Leeds, worked the down Queen of Scots, 12.05 ex-King's Cross the next day.

Copley Hill did not have sufficient main line work to enable the men to have regular engines, as was the case at King's Cross and Grantham, but they did have their own Copley Hill engines out and back on their main London workings, and as far as possible the same engines were kept regularly to the workings – "nominated engines" which is the next best thing to regular engines.

Although firing an A1 merely required an ability to put enough coal into the firebox, if it was not done carefully there could be a waste of steam from blowing off at the wrong time. Generally, the A1s were not such comfortable engines at speed as the A4s, particularly if the engine to tender drawbar was slack, as it was the leading tender wheels which contributed in considerable measure to steadying the back of the engine, consequently the brasses of these wheels also wore and had to be regularly replaced to keep the engines from being very rough. They were definitely uncomfortable at speed, and I never felt so happy coming down Stoke fast on an A1 as on an A4. An A4 had a gentle motion, rolling steadily, more like a ship, whereas an A1 jerked from side to side, and sometimes up and down as well.

With a boiler that could meet virtually any demands for steam, there were no problems when things were going wrong. One morning on the 7.50 am out of King's Cross, I had had to work quite hard, going down to Peterborough, and so took the precaution of making the fire up well as we were running in through Fletton. As soon as we opened up after going through Peterborough Station, I continued to build up what should have become a massive fire, only having a break whilst I dropped the scoop for Werrington troughs. As soon as we had got water I resumed shovelling, and never stopped until we were through Little Bytham. We were only running quite normally, with the usual load, and although I was able to take things more easily after Stoke Tunnel, I was still regularly shovelling away. By the time we stopped at Retford, I was having to reach back into the tender for the coal, and the fireman went in and pulled coal forward. I forget who the driver was – I think the engine was 60117 – but he asked me what I was doing with the coal! When he looked into the firebox, I think he was expecting to see a great box full and he was surprised to see a very light fire, to which I commented that I wondered what he was doing with the steam I was making! By the time we got to Leeds there was little coal left in the tender, yet it had been heaped full in the usual way when we left King's Cross. I went up to Copley Hill on the tram and when I got to the shed I went straight to the Shed Master, Jack Hardacre, and told him to look at the engine when she got to the shed. He was, of course, suitably horrified! He 'stopped' the engine for examination and found that she had got broken piston rings, and so was wasting the steam, which surprisingly had not been noticeable, as broken rings usually give a roar from the chimney, though A1s, with their double chimneys and soft blast, do not show such things as much as single chimney engines.

With the 19 King's Cross A4s doing the majority of the ATC runs, and working many of the trains it was most convenient for me to use to visit

Peterborough and Grantham, as well as Doncaster and Leeds on occasion, I rode regularly with all of them. One engine I wanted to experience was 60700, the old 10,000, but she was not ATC fitted and, in my time, was only at King's Cross for a short period. One day I was at Grantham and so was she, but I didnt't finish my business in time to go back up to King's Cross with her. I was lucky, because going down Stoke Bank she had a bad blow back due to a steam pipe failure in the smokebox, and the crew were slightly burnt. Likewise, I rarely rode on any of the Thompson Pacifics or the Peppercorn A2s, a few of which were at Peterborough.

The A4s with the corridor tenders were particularly enjoyable on the longer runs, as the fireman was able to go back into the train and replenish the tea cans or have a chat with the guard. On the Pullmans some extra refreshments were often provided for the loco crew, sandwiches or a block of ice-cream; not easy to eat on a footplate before it melted!

The story of the failure of 60007 *Sir Nigel Gresley*, with Bill Hoole, on the Tyne-Tees Pullman at Thirsk, on 22nd April 1954 is recounted by Peter Semmens in his book on Bill Hoole, "Engineman Extraordinary". This was the day when Bill got the V2 60981 from Grantham to King's Cross in 99 minutes, against the booked 110 minutes. When I got back to the office, I straightaway told Teddy Ker the story, and he in turn told J.S. "Jumper" Jones, the assistant MP Superintendent, who wanted to know what I was doing on such a train. It stopped me having any further nights out to Newcastle, and Teddy later apologised for dropping me into trouble!

My last trip with Bill and *Sir Nigel Gresley* before I left BR was on the 10.40am out of King's Cross, which was a relatively slow train to Grantham, returning with the up Flying Scotsman. Bill had arranged, quite unofficially, to take Ann Carter with him, an accomplished model maker in her own right, and daughter of the builder of a GN Atlantic which was a championship winner at the ME Exhibition. Bill had got friendly with the Carters there and this trip was the result. Once clear of Hitchin, he put Ann in the driving seat; she was quite competent in her handling of the engine, and the fireman kept his eye on the road whilst I looked after the fire. Bill proceeded to clear out the oil cupboard, putting all the oil bottles, etc., on the cab floor to clean, so what firing I had to do had to be done over and around them! Approaching St. Neots, we overhauled an Austerity, drifting along on the slow line, with the fireman looking out, and as he espied Ann, with pigtails hanging beneath her uniform cap over her overalls, we could see his eyes very nearly popping out! We stopped at St. Neots, and the Austerity trundled by, with the driver and fireman both looking out at us, and when we repassed them once agan, they were still all eyes on us!

Bill was not going to let Peterborough messroom get regaled with the story for nothing, so the next day when they passed the same crew at about the same spot, all eyes to see whether anyone else interesting was on the engine, they saw it was unoccupied! Bill and his mate had adjourned through the tender and watched the fun from the first coach! A

No. 60117 on Up Queen of Scots Pullman, passing Peterborough.

good thing that the travelling public doesn't know some of the things which go on up front, though in those days it was mostly quite harmless.

Although Bill was probably the driver on the East Coast who could most be relied upon to make time, or run early, others could give good runs too. On 24th June 1954 George Mattock, with 60118 on the up Leeds flyer, left Leeds two minutes late, got to Doncaster one minute early (with four coaches) but left five minutes late. Signals at Counthorpe, Little Bytham and Essendine, a 45 mph PWC at Muskham, 20 PWC at Lolham, and 40 PWC at Connington meant we were four or five minutes late all the way to Hitchin, but climbing to Potters Bar this was all picked up and we were two minutes early at Finsbury Park and King's Cross, just what everyone wanted. Percy Heavens with the 60015 on the Junior Scotsman (5.16pm King's Cross arrival) on the 13th July, converted a nine minutes late start from Peterborough to four minutes late at Potters Bar, and one minute late on arrival.

On the up Leeds Flyer on 20th July, E. Brown on 60123 converted six minutes late at Newark and Grantham to 4½ minutes late at Peterborough, three minutes late leaving Hitchin, ¾ minutes early at Potters Bar, and two minutes early into King's Cross.

On 17th November 1954 I travelled with G. Hannan on 60133 on the up Yorkshire Pullman, an unusual train for me to use, but I had been talking about ATC to Bradford Mutual Improvement Class the night before. We dropped two minutes at Doncaster attaching the Hull portion and were five minutes late leaving and had only picked up a quarter of a minute to Grantham, but in spite of signals approaching Peterborough, were only ½ minute late passing. Hitchin was passed ½ minute early, and in spite of PWCs at Langley, Digswell and Potters Bar, were two minutes early at Hatfield, 2½ minutes early at Potters Bar and six minutes early on arrival at King's Cross.

Looking at the bare figures of the notebook, it is impossible to convey what it all meant in terms of effort, frustration and relief. PWCs could be planned for, it meant that it was a time to put on both injectors. On an A1 this needed the water level to have been allowed to run down a bit, but with an engine that was not steaming too freely, it was an opportunity to regain a bit of water, keeping the fire going as much as possible with the blower. Signal checks were different. They were unexpected and could create considerable difficulties or relief for the fireman. If it occurred in the middle of a hard stretch, with a good engine with a big fire it would be difficult to prevent the engine blowing off, and the boiler would soon be full. If signals actually stopped the train, it was difficult to keep the fire in a good state ready for getting away again, not knowing how long this would be, though with the free steaming double chimney engines the problem was easier, and all that was necessary once the right away came, was to shovel in a bit more coal, and it would soon burn through and the boiler would be producing the steam required. With a less free steaming engine, it was an opportunity to build up the water and steam to the maximum possible, in the hope that the signal came off just when the boiler was full, or the fire had to be quietened down and then when the signal came off some of the advantage was lost accelerating the train and getting the fire hot again.

It was all part of the work on the footplate which made it so interesting. It could be hard work, but few runs involved continuous hard work for very long, and it was not heavy if done properly. Many of the older drivers regularly took a turn on the shovel for a spell, it was a way to keep themselves in trim, and they exemplified the easy way to do it, by bringing experience and deft use of the shovel rather than brute strength and large shovels full of coal – not that such was very possible with LNER flap doors. It gave senior firemen the experience they needed for the day when they would become a passed fireman and have to drive themselves. Nevertheless, footplate work was a job which had many disadvantages, particularly with the irregular hours, and it was essentially a vocation.

To my mind, there was nothing quite like an A4, particularly with a double chimney, but even with the King's Cross fastened blastpipe, they were good to ride and were comfortable at speed, far more than an A1, which was hard and uncomfortable, especially if slack between engine and tender. An A3, or even a good V2, could be a pleasure too, if not having to be pushed too much. B1s on heavy work were a challenge, and could be rough, but the smaller engines I worked on were mostly well within their capabilities and gave much less of a challenge.

The enjoyment I was getting on engines was one of the negative factors when it came to leaving BR, but I could see the writing on the wall for steam, and my days of intensive travel for ATC purposes were over. Father had retired and was moving south, so my fun on the B1s was also diminishing. Nevertheless, I managed to have a few unofficial runs with Bill Hoole before he retired and moved to Wales, and then I had a few trips on 4472 before she went to America. Firing is like riding a bicycle, once learnt, it is never forgotten, and on occasions when I have been privileged to wield the shovel on any of the preserved engines, I find it just the same as it always was, except that muscles tell me after a while that they are not used to such exertions. Nevertheless, I find that after firing for a few days that they are getting back to form, though I would not like to tackle what I did when younger!

CHAPTER IX

Wales

In Chapter V, I referred to my meeting with Bill Harvey at Stratford in 1951 and the decision to spend a holiday together that July, working on the Talyllyn Railway. Bill told me that he was staying at Rhowniar, then a young people's hostel, with a few double rooms which were let privately. Bill travelled from Birmingham by the Cambrian Coast Express, but I had a 350cc BSA motor cycle. Originally a small machine had been a necessity so that I could get backwards and forwards between Doncaster and Lincoln on Friday and Sunday evenings, as suitable trains were virtually non-existent, and petrol was still on ration. I had virtually never been to Wales before, and was bowling along the road from Aberdovey, when a shout from Bill sitting on a stile by the roadside saved me from driving past, as I had not appreciated that Rhowniar was some way out of the town of Towyn.

Although I knew of Bill Harvey's reputation as a sound practical engineer, we did not really know each other, but apart from our railway and locomotive interests, we soon found that we had a common interest in boats, particularly rowing. Bill rowed with the Yare Rowing Club, and our association led to the Oakley participating in more than one regatta at Norwich.

On that first visit to the Talyllyn Railway in 1951 we of course went straight down to Pendre shed on the Sunday morning to introduce ourselves to Tom Rolt and David Curwen. In those days little happened on Sundays, and there were no trains running, so we went off together on the bike to look at the various Talyllyn Railway stations and to walk the top section, from Abergynolwyn to the quarry including seeing the crude but effective watering arrangements by the head of the Abergynolwyn village incline. We then learnt the vagaries of Welsh licensing when we partook of a (dry) lunch at Dolgellau before heading northwards to Maentwrog and a look at the Festiniog Railway.

On that first visit we worked with David Curwen on no. 3, one of the ex-Corris Railway engines, then un-named, but now *Sir Haydn*. There were virtually no facilities at Pendre, apart from a blacksmith's hearth and a screwing machine. *Dolgoch* was maintaining the train service, driven by John Snell with the old TR coaches. Each journey was an adventure, and when the train left Pendre we always wondered whether it would come back when it should. The track was literally held in place by

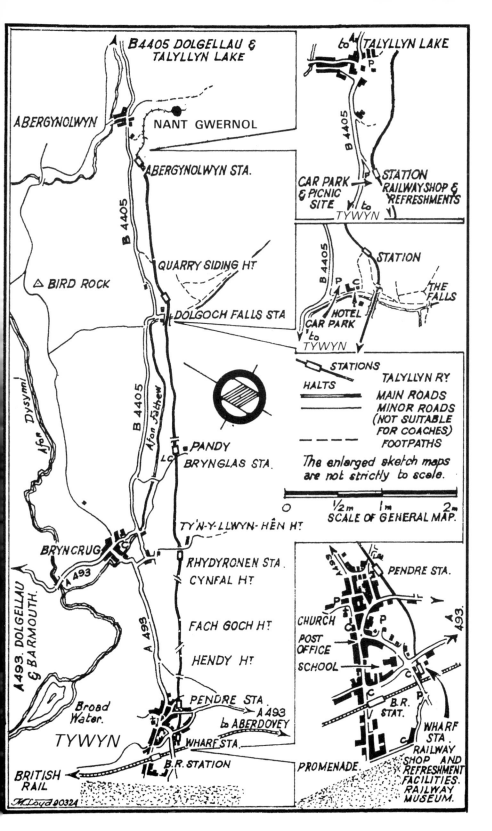

The Talyllyn Railway today.

No. 3 inside Tywyn Pendre works. 1951

the turf, and the joints between the rails were in many cases still held together by joint chairs. Travelling on the engine was an exciting business, watching the rails lift out of the turf and sometimes away from the joint chairs, and hoping that they would drop back into the right place! Usually they did, but occasionally they did not, whereupon a crunching noise usually ensued as engine and/or coaches tried to run on the turf. Then it was a question of finding a few strong men, a rail, a sleeper or two, and by

106

Tom Rolt (in straw hat) with David Curwen and the author (on the footplate of no. 3) at Tywyn Pendre on 21st July 1951.

simple application of levers, rerailing the appropriate vehicles. The difficulty was trying to get the rails back into position under the vehicles to some semblance of the proper 2'3" gauge.

We finished off a few minor details on no. 3, and on the Wednesday, *Dolgoch* ventured into the back road to the "Works" to pull out both the ex-Corris engines, whereupon we put no. 3 in steam and did various

107

further jobs found necessary. On the Saturday, David Curwen, Bill and I took her up towards Abergynolwyn, but then we learnt, the hard way, that her wheel treads were narrower than those of *Dolgoch*, when she dropped between the rails not very far up the line. Consequently, although she was available as a standby, she could not be used until the track was relaid and kept reasonably reliably to gauge.

The TR main line, from the footplate of Dolgoch, *when propelling a wagon, on 23rd May 1952.*

By 1952 volunteers had relaid the track at Wharf Station to give a proper run round loop, and had got no. 4, *Edward Thomas*, ready for service, giving the old lady, *Dolgoch*, a welcome relief from every day service.

Bill and I arranged to spend Coronation Week, 1953, at Towyn, and to help with reassembly of *Dolgoch* after some essential repairs. We re-fitted the axle boxes to the journals and horns, and rewheeled and re-assembled her. We also refitted some of the fittings which had been overhauled, including the blowdown valve on the back of the firebox under the cab floor. On the Sunday we took her for a quiet run with one of the ex-Penrhyn open quarryman's coaches, but one of the driving axle boxes was running much too warm for comfort, and we had to take the wheels out again on the Monday and rebed the brasses.

In our work, we had also learnt a lot about *Dolgoch's* peculiar motion. Allans Straight Link inside is not unusual, but on Dolgoch the eccentrics

From left to right – Vic Mitchell, Dai Jones, Dolgoch, *John Snell and Bill Harvey.*

are on the leading axle, with the eccentric rods going back to the links, which then had long intermediate rods going round the leading axle forward to the valve spindle.

We had been concerned at the amount of steam coming apparently from the blow down valve joint, and after we had got her wheeled again I was endeavouring to find exactly what was leaking – the plates were wet even under no pressure – and I found that the water was coming from the actual back plate itself. Digging with a penknife revealed not just a crack, but a veritable slot going through to just above the foundation ring. It was only an accumulation of scale on the foundation ring that had kept the water in the boiler, yet she had recently successfully undergone a hydraulic test. Now I had revealed a real hole, large enough to pass my complete penknife into the water space!

Help was sought from the Glaslyn Foundry to weld up the fracture, and I arranged to drive up to Towyn for a weekend at the beginning of July, to replace the wheels and rods once again.

In July 1954, the army were relaying track above Dolgoch, and we were entrusted with no. 3 to work PW trains for them. Bill and I were staying at Dolgoch, so we "stabled" the engine there overnight and lit her up there in the morning, visiting Towyn with the engine in the evening to collect fuel, stores, etc. By that time the track was in a more secure state allowing no. 3 to be used more regularly. In September, I took Bill Hoole with me to Towyn for a weekend, introducing him not only to the beauties

No. 4 at Nant Gwernol on 30th September 1952.

of Wales, but also the fun of working on a railway run by volunteers, as well as the attractions of the narrow gauge.

On that first visit to the Festiniog Railway in 1951, Bill Harvey and I went along the bottom road from the Oakley Arms Hotel in Maentwrog towards Blaenau, parked my bike by the roadside and climbed the hillside to find the Festiniog track. We had failed to look at the contours on the map to realise how far up it was! This was one of the best preserved sections of the Festiniog Railway track, and we walked up as far as the tunnel, balancing on the rails through some of the wet cuttings; two people locking arms and shoulders can easily walk one on each 2 foot gauge rail! Seeing the FR track, we both commented that we felt that this was the railway we should be working on. Bill walked back through Garnedd Tunnel to Tanybwlch, whilst I walked down to pick up the bike to collect him, and we went on to look at Portmadoc and Boston Lodge,

Bill Hoole with no. 4 at Tywyn Wharf.

which convinced us even more, that here was a once fine railway, basically much better built and maintained than the Talyllyn Railway.

A few weeks later, a letter appeared in the Railway Gazette, concerning
a scheme to revive the Festiniog Railway. I wrote in reply, and was told
that a meeting would be held at the Bristol Railway Circle's room on
8 September. I went along to that meeting, and found several others
there, and although called for 2.30pm, the schoolboy, Leonard Heath
Humphrys who had called it, came in about twenty minutes late.
Apologising for being late, he launched straight into some dissertations
on the costs of concrete sleepers for relaying track and various other
matters regarding restoring the railway, but little regarding how we were
going to get permission to do it. Of those at that meeting, Leonard Heath
Humphrys, now a Festiniog Society Vice President, John Bate, now
Chief Engineer of the Talyllyn Railway, and Vic Mitchell, the publisher

of this book, and myself, were all present at a celebratory dinner in 1983 after the opening of Blaenau Festiniog new station.

From an early stage, it was obvious that the only way in which we could hope to achieve any revival was to take over the company by buying out the principal shareholders, including the National Westminster Bank, who held a large holding of debentures as security for a bank loan which they had given for the widening of the Britannia Bridge at Portmadoc for the connection of the Welsh Highland Railway when it came to Portmadoc in 1923. However, the Festiniog Railway Company were not prepared to let us use the name 'Festiniog Railway' to publicise what we were trying to do.

The Festiniog Railway Company at that time was still trading, with receipts from the slates worked over its lines at Blaenau Ffestiniog by the quarries – Maenofferen, Votty and Bowydd, also rents coming in from its houses and various wayleaves, which enabled it to continue to pay its Manager, Robert Evans, who had been with the company for a lifetime, as well as continue to pay part of the loan interest – on paper they were paying it all, but at an increasing overdraft. The Bank realised that the slate business was declining, so that the future was uncertain, and were prepared to sell their debentures for £2,000. The Davies' family wanted another £1,000. £3,000 to buy a derelict railway with a dozen houses sounds little by today's monetary values, but it can be related more when I say that I was earning £450 a year, which was quite a reasonable salary! Few people at that time believed it was possible to operate a railway with volunteers, and industrial archeological preservation was virtually unheard of, so how we were going to raise the sort of money to acquire control of the Company was a problem on which we spent a lot of time trying to find a solution.

Whilst working at Tilbury, I had met Bill Broadbent, then railway representative of Vacuum Oil Company, now Mobil, regarding oil supplies in the stores, particularly barrel pumps, and over lunch at Tilbury Riverside we had discovered mutual interests, including the Festiniog. I persuaded him to join us and at the first, and only, meeting of interested people, held at the SLS headquarters opposite Kensington Olympia on 22 April 1952, we made Bill Broadbent chairman of the organisation.

We looked at various ways of raising the money required to purchase the company, but it was obvious we could not do it by appeals when we could not use the name "Festiniog Railway". The only solution seemed to be to try to find someone willing to sink money into the scheme. One of our members, Tom King, worked at Finchley Council with Les Smith, and he, with an old army pal, Trevor Bailey, in turn worked with Alan Pegler in running various special trains using unusual engines. Alan Pegler was persuaded to look at the FR, became interested, and agreed to put up the money.

At a meeting on a cold, foggy Saturday afternoon, 2 January 1954, at Finchley Town Baths, Les Smith and Trevor Bailey told us that Alan Pegler was prepared to buy up the Company if we would form a Society to

Inside Boston Lodge erecting shop in 1952 with the new boiler for Prince *behind its frames, and* Taliesin *in the background.*

help him run the railway. This was not quite what we had originally wanted, but we felt that after over two years of frustration, this was going to be the best way to get the railway going again, and we accepted. Bill Broadbent conducted the negotiations with Alan Pegler and on 24 June, the latter took over the company and opened a new bank account, with the obligation to continue to employ – and pay – Robert Evans. We formed the Society into a company limited by guarantee to give it formal status and avoid liability to its members, and started to try to attract funds and volunteers.

CHAPTER X

The Festiniog comes to life

During a wet spell of the summer of 1954, a party from St. Pauls School, under Mike Elvy, started to clear the jungle blocking the tracks above Boston Lodge, and in September, Bill Harvey and I stayed for a few days at Portmadoc before going on to Towyn for the Talyllyn A.G.M. We arranged for Morris Jones to join us at Boston Lodge to show us what was what. Morris had served his apprenticeship there, gone to sea, and then been called back to try to restore some order to the chaotic locomotive position in the 20s, and remained at Boston Lodge until just after the railway closed in 1946. He had a smallholding just off the Caernarfon Road towards Garn Dolbenmaen, and was also working part time for the Talyllyn Railway. With his help and guidance, we set to work on the Simplex petrol locomotive cleaning up and repairing the ignition system, checking it over, and after putting some petrol into the tank, with some frantic winding of the starting handle, coaxed the engine into life. We set off down the Works Yard, thinking we could go over to Portmadoc by rail for a drink for ourselves and fuel for the Simplex, but when we opened the Works Yard gates, those hopes were rudely dashed, as there was a good six inches of sand covering the tracks. We spent the afternoon digging a way through and pole shunting remains of some quarryman's coaches blocking the way, but by the end of the day had succeeded in making a few wheels turn once again.

That night, back at the Commercial Hotel where we were staying, David Owen, the owner, sat and talked with us as we finished our dinner, and when he learnt what we were doing, became most interested and immediately fetched the local newspaper reporter, Herbert Thomas, who arranged to come over to Boston Lodge next day with Robert Evans as well, to record the start of the revival of the Festiniog, and give us some publicity. So started a friendship with two of our staunchest supporters in the area.

During that winter we arranged with scrap merchants to clear away much of the redundant vehicles at Harbour Station to raise money to help purchase sleepers to repair the track, and also to engage staff. We were able to get a young lad, Arwyn Morgan, then finishing his apprenticeship,

114

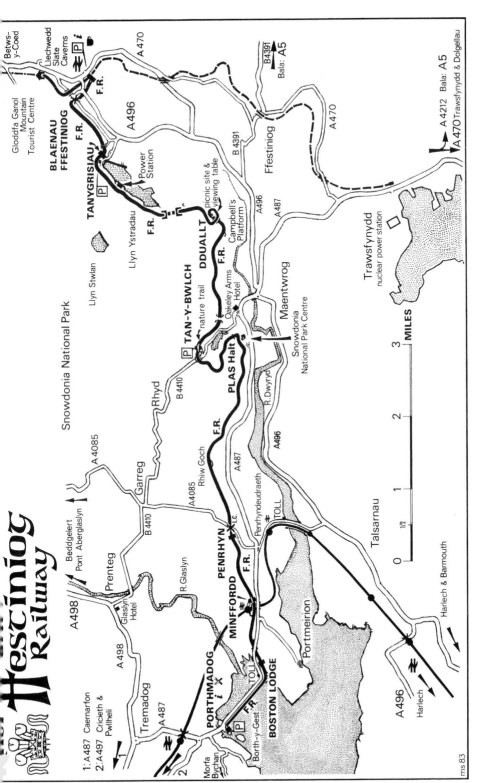

The Ffestiniog Railway today.

ms 83

Boston Lodge works yard with John Bate and Bill Harvey in July 1954.

to come to work with Morris Jones, to get Boston Lodge Works function-
ing and resume work started years before on reassembling *Prince*, which
had been under repair when the railway closed, and for which a brand
new boiler was sitting in the Works.

Just above Boston Lodge Halt, the embankment had collapsed into a
small culvert, and so that we could go up the line with the Simplex, we
made a crib of timbers to support the tracks. The tracks to Minffordd and
Penrhyn were completely blocked by brambles. We charged at them
until, usually, we slipped to a stand, and then, having created a clearing,
would put some sand on the rails and have another charge. Occasionally,
rocks or even an unseen turnout, would cause a derailment, when we
would have to delve into the brambles to get the machine back onto the
rails. At Pen Cefn we had to remove a wall where a neighbour had extended their garden onto the FR track. This work was done entirely by
volunteers, who we arranged would come to work on certain weekends
when I arranged to come up from London.

If I was coming up alone from London to Portmadoc, or with another
railwayman, I travelled overnight from Euston. With luck and if the trains
were on time, I caught the early train from Bangor so that I was into
Portmadoc soon after 6.00 am, and then I went to the Commercial Bakery
for a warm corner until the hotel opened. If, as often happened, the

116

Crewe train was late, there was another train which got into Portmadoc just in time for breakfast. Sunday evening, it was the 6.30 pm bus to Caernarvon, another bus to Bangor, and train thence to Euston, which was reached at about 3.30 am. I always took my car and left it at King's Cross, so that I could get back to Wanstead, where I was in digs, and get to bed for a while before going to work. Sometimes, I drove down by road, but before the time of motorways, it was a long slow journey, with the alternatives of heavy traffic and frustration on the A5, or less tiring but longer journeys other ways.

Boston Lodge had never had mains electricity, and all that we could afford then was a normal domestic single phase supply. Although this was of no use for driving machines, it enabled handtools, even a small welder, to be used, as well as handlamps, which were a great improvement on the flare lamps which we otherwise had to use. I remember the thrill of coming back on the Simplex one Saturday afternoon, and finding the erecting shop a relative blaze of light after a gang of electrical volunteers had installed the first wiring.

On 6 November, a celebration was held to present a clock to Robert Evans to mark his sixty years with the Company, 25 of them as Manager. However, he could not reconcile himself to the Railway being revived,

The narrow gauge/standard gauge crossing at Blaenau Ffestiniog, in May 1952.

117

Bill Harvey ponders on the Blaenau Ffestiniog booking office sign, in May 1952.

and thought we were all quite mad, particularly myself and some of the younger volunteers.

By March 1955, the Simplex reached the GW station at Blaenau and it was possible for a train, of sorts, to travel throughout from Portmadoc to Blaenau Festiniog. Nevertheless, any journey was an adventure; up to Cei Mawr the sleepers were in very uncertain condition, though the heavy chaired track joined by big and solid fishplates, did hold the rails much more securely than was the case at Towyn. There was a more or less complete absence of keys, yet we rarely suffered a derailment other than because of rocks or bits of tree on the line which could not be seen under the general growth. The Simplex itself was not without its own excitements; its petrol consumption was measured more in gallons per mile than miles per gallon, so I made arrangements to use T.V.O. (Tractor Vapourising Oil) which was virtually paraffin used by farm tractors before the universal use of diesels. Once the engine had warmed up on petrol, it was changed over to TVO – an additional small tank had been provided for the petrol – but if the engine should stop, it would not normally restart on paraffin, and then there was the problem of flooding the petrol through into the carburettor. The engine normally functioned with plenty of bangs and sparks from its exhaust, which caused some hilarity to those accompanying it. A big problem on a line such as the FR was that the starting handle went in at the side. With the FRs limited clearances, it was impossible to get the handle in at many places, and at others, even if it could be got into position, it was extremely difficult to get sufficient effort to it to effectively swing such a heavy engine. Nevertheless, for all its

Presentation to Robert Evans on 6th November 1954.

Back row: Messrs. Garraway, Gilbert, W. Smith, Davies, Broadbent, Smallman, Nicholson, Routly, Williams, Bellamy.
Seated: Mrs. Williams, Mrs. Evans, Messrs. Heath-Humphrys, Evans, Bailey, L. Smith, Pegler.

faults, that engine started the FRs revival, and for many years it has continued to give very useful service.

The driving chains broke with monotonous regularity and had to be retrieved, mended and refitted. They had worn and stretched and eventually had more bolted links than proper ones and eventually we had to find a replacement, but they were an obsolete type. We were fortunate in finding a baby Simplex abandoned on the track bed of the old Welsh Highland Railway near Portmadoc, which we raided to provide a spare gearbox and half size engine (two cylinder version instead of four), as it used many similar components.

There was one memorable night, in January 1955, when we left the Simplex in the woods and travelled home by bus, as a big end had failed. On the following day, Sunday, we managed to get it back to Boston Lodge with the help of gravity and a little manpower, for the ancient engine to be repaired by Morris Jones and Arwyn, since without it we were totally without motive power.

Having got a way through to Blaenau, we set about making the first mile out of Portmadoc, over the causeway, known as the Cob, fit for passenger services. Pre-war, the Company had bought some locally sawn timber for sleepers as well as second hand ones from the GWR. These were delivered to Minffordd, and the bottom gang, who looked after the stretch from Portmadoc up to Cei Mawr, kept the local timber sleepers, which were lighter and cleaner, for themselves, and sent the ex-GWR ones to the other gangs. These untreated sleepers had a very short life and after about twenty years they were more or less useless, not only completely failing to hold the chair spikes, but in many cases not even able to carry any load, and the worst of them were those on the Cob, many of which were only pulp. Consequently, before trains could run, it was essential to replace at least three or four sleepers a rail length.

With the intention to resume train services, the directors were looking for someone to succeed Robert Evans as General Manager, and I intimated that I would like to be considered. Sir Brian Robertson, then Chairman of BR had announced his modernisation programme, basically the phasing out of steam and its replacement with diesels, in which I could raise no interest whatsoever. I realised also that I had either to get more involved with the FR, or step to one side and let someone else take over. Most thought me quite mad, and I felt a little guilty at taking on such a task after Father had spent so much on sending me to Cambridge. However, as he said, because I had got qualifications behind me, I could afford to do something I wanted to do and, if it didn't work out, I could get back again. In subsequent years many of those people were to envy me getting out of BR when I did, and enjoying the rewards of achievement of ambitions. By the time I actually moved to Portmadoc the future of the FR was looking a little uncertain, but I felt a truncated line of ten miles into the hills could still be an interesting proposition. In fact, this may not have been such a bad thing, because the strike which took place on BR soon after I left showed that railways were dispensable, and to my mind did tremendous harm to the future of railways in Britain.

By July, plans were being made for inspection by Colonel MacMullen of the Railway Inspectorate, and for train services to start from Portmadoc to Boston Lodge. *Prince* was not ready, and though the track had had some new sleepers put in and was probably better than that which the TR was running on, it was still very poor. Although the carriage brakes had been overhauled, they could not be tested until *Prince* was ready and to provide a means of creating vacuum as the Simplex could not do this. However, Colonel MacMullen had been very considerate to the TR and he was likewise to the FR, so that from what he saw on 21 July 1955 he agreed to allow trains to run, subject to speed not exceeding ten miles per hour. On 23 July, train services started using Simplex and the two freshly painted coaches.

Frantic efforts were made to get *Prince* completed, even more so when Simplex's magneto started to object to continuous passenger duty, and had annoying bouts of failure, so that trains had to be cancelled. *Prince* crossed the Cob on 2nd August, the anniversary of the railway closing, and took over the passenger service the next day, and ran until the end of the season. Unfortunately, the vacuum brakes on the trains were found not to work properly, as the replacement rolling rings had not quite the right clearances, but at least the train could be piped together, and the guard had his brake valve. There were no run round facilities at Boston Lodge, so the train had to be shunted by chain, the engine going up into the yard, and the points being changed between engine and train, so that the coaches went along the main line. This had its embarassments, on one occasion the coaches overran a bit too far and tried to take the tender with them, pulling it nearly over, but, fortunately, not completely. A little water tank on top of one of the gatepost pillars at Boston Lodge gave a temporary water supply.

We had not dared to publicise resumption of services until everything was certain and Colonel MacMullen had given his permission, so publicity had been minimal, but by the time trains stopped running on 24th September, some 11,000 people had made 20,000 journeys, back and forth over the Cob.

During the following winter the Society started to get itself better organised, with groups forming in some of the more populous areas. The Midland Group did a lot of the clearing work of the track between Boston Lodge and Minffordd, and in January, Will Jones, who lived in Tanybwlch Station House, and had been the Ganger when the railway closed, joined the staff to assist with resleepering and other work to restore the track.

During the winter much effort went into cutting up more redundant wagons for scrap, to raise much needed cash. I would spend much time during the week cutting up as many as I could into appropriately sized pieces, and then volunteers at the weekend would help load it into BR wagons. Much needed first aid repairs on all the buildings got started – some are still in need of work to bring them fully up to necessary standards – and work on providing a telephone system commenced.

Another brake and compartment coach was repainted, no. 11, largely

A. Pegler (centre) and the Smith brothers.

because it needed the least work to get it into traffic, and it was turned round so that there was a brake van at each end of the train. This coach had one compartment which had upholstered backs to the seats, so some bus seats were acquired for it, and it was put into traffic as a first class compartment, which immediately proved extremely popular, even at 50 per cent higher fare – three shillings (15 pence) return, to Minffordd, as against two shillings (ten pence) for the third class fare. The next coach to be repaired was no. 17, which included a proper first class compartment, so extra effort was put into restoring this vehicle with its upholstery intact, providing it with additional similar bus seats which proved even more popular.

Train services were started to Minffordd on 19 May 1956 and operated daily until 22 September. As has always been the case, June proved a difficult month to maintain the service. Ellis Jones, who lived in Minffordd Station House, acted as guard and booking clerk, whilst on some days I had to act as both driver and fireman. There were four trains each way in the afternoons, and the number of passengers were few, though on one occasion when I thought we were going to have an empty train I got caught out! As there were no passengers at Minffordd for the last train to Portmadoc, I thought we could leave the coaches there and I could go straight to Boston Lodge instead of going to Portmadoc, and back to Minffordd to take Ellis home. Drifting down to Boston Lodge Halt, I was dismayed to find a lady waiting for the train! Not to disappoint her, I explained what had happened, and took her to Portmadoc on the engine! She was quite thrilled with the trip, but it taught me never to cancel a train

Prince pulling out tree roots in Cutting Gwlyb, 1957.

Prince on the Britannia Bridge collecting rails in September 1958.

and in fact in all the years we have run trains, I never recall one occasion when there has not been a passenger on a train for some part of its round trip.

The Directors were very anxious to see one of the Double Fairlies for which the Festiniog was particularly famous, restored to service. *Taliesin* was in Boston Lodge partly stripped for overhaul, and it was arranged for staff from the Vulcan Foundry, Newton le Willows, which had just become part of the English Electric Group, but had been one of the great steam locomotive builders, to come to Boston Lodge to do the necessary work. Frank Basnett and Bill Plumpton aided by others from time to time did much of the work, with Michael Bacon visiting occasionally to provide general supervision. Michael was an old Eastleigh man, and later moved to Peterborough where he was closely involved with the formation of the Nene Valley Railway from Wansford to the outskirts of Peterborough. *Taliesin* ran trial runs on Sunday 2nd September and ran the full day's service on Wednesday 5th September.

The passenger service ceased on 22nd September; by this time 21,000 people had made 39,000 journeys, a satisfying result.

For 1957, it was planned to restore services to Penrhyndeudraeth which necessitated a loop being constructed, not altogether easy in the limited space available. No. 12 was modified to provide a small sales counter and buffet car, though only serving bottles of 'pop', chocolates, guide books, etc., and no. 11 was arranged to run next to it, van to van, with the brake pipes modified, and fall plates provided, so that it was possible to walk from one coach to the other. So was started the idea of Festiniog corridor trains, and driving *Prince* that summer, looking at the blank end of no. 11, I felt it should have windows in it for people to see the views better from the train. 1957 also saw the start of evening trains, four nights a week in July and August.

During the summer of 1957, a great effort was made to properly clear the track onwards to Tanybwlch. During the long evenings in June and July, *Prince* was often taken above Penrhyn and used to haul out the roots left in the track after the initial way through had been cleared, and with the larger gangs of volunteers in August this work continued apace. Keith Catchpole and his boys from Enfield School achieved the final clearance so that on a very wet Friday evening, 6th September, *Prince*, no. 23 and Buffet Car no. 12, were taken up to Tanybwlch.

During the following winter, great effort was put into resleepering the track from Penrhyn. to Cei Mawr, the last length with many of the old locally sawn softwood sleepers. Above Cei Mawr only one or two odd sleepers were replaced, and a few keys put in, for train services to start at Easter 1958. Meanwhile, at Boston Lodge I made the rebuild of no. 11 as an Observation Car my primary winter task, whilst overhaul of nos. 18 and 22 progressed.

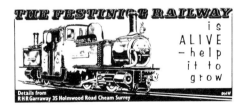

THE FESTINIOG RAILWAY is ALIVE – help it to grow

Details from
R H R Garraway 35 Holmwood Road Cheam Surrey

CHAPTER XI

Tanybwlch

With train services again running to Tanybwlch, a lot of people were thinking that since the FR had moved forward a bit each year, with the big step in 1958 more than doubling the mileage, so it should keep on and do a further step the next year. I realised that we were living on a knife edge with the track, and although we had put in a lot of new sleepers, particularly on some stretches, there were an awful lot of old sleepers which had little hold on the spikes, and, more particularly, for the three miles from Cei Mawr to Tanybwlch, which included a lot of fairly sharp curves, we had hardly renewed any, nor had we done much else. When Colonel MacMullen made his inspection, I got him to emphasise the need for consolidation before we tried to go further, and this he made in his report, thereby taking the responsibility for 'staying put' off both myself and the Board.

A lot of us expected that with only half the train service of previous years, our passenger numbers would be down. However, 1958 was the first of many seasons where, during the peak weeks of August, we were overwhelmed by the numbers of people wanting to travel. In August, we hastily got together the best of the four wheeled coaches and, together with the four wheeled no. 1 Brake van, made up a relief train for *Prince* to haul initially to Penrhyn for coach tour passengers, but in fact virtually always to Tanybwlch. On one of its first runs, Colonel MacMullen's daughter was travelling on it, and as would happen on such an occasion, one of the four wheelers derailed at 3 Gates Level Crossing. We never did find out the cause, even some years later when *Linda* derailed at the same spot, though on that occasion we did find a defect with the engine springing. The Colonel was very sympathetic over the incident, and consoled us with the fact that inexplicable derailments with four wheeled vehicles had caused troubles in India and elsewhere.

In 1958 the FR carried 33,000 people, making 60,000 journeys. Nine years later, 124,000 people made 221,000 journeys. By that time virtually all the carriages we had taken over had been restored or replaced by equivalents, and we had started on a programme of building new carriages, but the August crowds were just as much a problem. In 1960 the passenger journeys passed the 100,000 mark, in 1967 they topped 200,000.

The ten years of running to Tanybwlch was the period when the Railway really started to become established as a major tourist attraction of the area, not only that, but it was proving, along with the Talyllyn, the Welsh-pool and Llanfair, the Bluebell, the Keighley and Worth Valley, etc., that railways of all gauges could be run on a 'do it yourself' basis, using volunteers to a greater or lesser extent.

I mentioned that at the time I actually left BR and moved to Portmadoc, the FRs future looked even less hopeful. This was because a House of Lords Select Committee had just decided that it was quite impractical to restore the Festiniog in its entirety, for which there was no need, as there was a perfectly adequate bus service, and that it was only a plaything for schoolboys and old men, for whom there would still be ten miles to play with. This was the Select Committee enquiring into the Electricity Authority's plan to build a pumped storage scheme near Tanygrisiau, Blaenau Ffestiniog, which would flood the route of the railway from the Moelwyn Tunnel to Tanygrisiau Station. Nevertheless, a David and Goliath battle started between the little impecunious Festiniog Railway and the giant national electricity authority, a battle which the Railway was eventually to win in a peculiarly roundabout British compromise, aided by the dedication of hundreds of volunteers. That is a story in itself which has been well documented elsewhere, but part of the deviation route which the Railway built to get round the obstacle included a three hundred yard tunnel, and "Construction News" likened it to the "Chunnel", and said that we had built our tunnel when we weren't sure where the finance was coming from to finish the job and complete the whole scheme, so why could not the Chunnel be built and finished?

The Tanybwlch decade, and the following one, too, were years of very hard work by a dedicated band of volunteers and permanent staff. To try to carry the passengers wanting to travel, we were trying to restore more coaches, as well as run more trains, but they in turn were imposing an ever greater strain on the track! Some of the wheels were worn, with deep sharp flanges, so that on the worn double head rails, they were striking the chairs which were in turn breaking. Naturally, this was mostly happening on the more solid sleepers, so that the hold on the rails by the few good sleepers was diminished. The need was to get the whole railway resleepered, but there was also a need to replace all the old 'S' chairs which were breaking so fast, as well as replace much of the older double head rail. A little rail, ex the Welsh Highland and from the tunnel did help, but we did not have the finance to purchase rail or chairs, as well as for the other things necessary, and in the early 1960s, I lived in dread of a derailment occurring and trains having to stop running whilst the track was repaired. This would have exacerbated the problem by reducing the revenue and precluding the purchase of vital materials. In 1961 there was a derailment of *Linda,* the worst that has happened in recent years, though this was not altogether due to the track, but in many ways this marked the turning point in the track conditions in that we were at last able to eliminate the really bad places. We know that on one occasion, one wheel of one coach actually dropped in, but, fortunately rerailed itself. A friend was in the coach concerned and told us of something

Boiler and new tanks for Merddyn Emrys *in Boston Lodge yard, June 1950.*

peculiar, and when we examined both track and wheels, we could see what had happened. Maybe it had happened before, or elsewhere; that we did not discover.

It was not only the track which was being overworked, but the engines as well. As the traffic grew and more carriages were restored and built, the trains became bigger and more, and larger, engines were needed. What was worse, the peak summer services needed every engine and carriage to be available, but no sooner was one engine overhauled and ready for service, than another had to be withdrawn. This meant that if any defect occurred, someone probably had to work late into the night to repair it ready for trains the next day. Such are the joys of running little railways on a shoestring!

In 1958, the plan was to run the heavier trains with *Taliesin,* using *Prince* on the lighter ones, but once the relief 'Flea' started, this necessitated two engines being available. As more carriages became available in following years so both the main train and the 'Flea' became heavier, and the latter went into the timetable together with a morning train for certain regular coach tours. In 1962 the timetable was recast to provide a peak season service to Tanybwlch with two trains, crossing at Minffordd, and although the trains did have rather long layovers at Portmadoc, it provided a better service with more frequent and regular departures. I believe that the secret of success with the Festiniog has been the policy of providing a reasonably frequent service of trains. This needs both a sufficient number, as well as sufficiently powerful engines, and although

Linda *arriving at Minffordd Yard on 14th July 1962, with Mr Parry, the foreman in charge.*

Prince was invaluable in the early years, trains were out-growing his capabilities. Five coaches should really be his limit, and, even today, though modernisation has enabled him to pull heavier trains, his bearings are not adequate if regularly overloaded, and wear occurs rapidly.

To help cope with the increasing traffic, it was agreed that *Merddyn Emrys,* the other Fairlie, should be overhauled. This necessitated a set of new tanks, but fortunately good friends at John Somers Steelworks – then still privately owned – arranged to weld some up for us and in 1961 we actually had two Fairlies running, but no *Prince* as he had been withdrawn

The Lynton and Barnstaple coach dismantled at Snapper on 1st May 1959.

Reassembling the L and B coach, with new steel underframe for no. 11 in the foreground. 12th February 1962.

for fitting new cylinders, as well as boiler work. In 1962 we thought the position would be better once *Prince* was ready for traffic, but *Merddyn Emrys* developed problems with the crown stays, owing to the ferrules corroding, (these are distance pieces separating the firebox crown from the girder bars). Once trains started running, work at Boston Lodge always slows down, as people became involved not only in running trains but also in maintaining engines and carriages in traffic, but with the help of volunteers, *Prince* was eventually ready for the peak season traffic, if slightly late. Taliesin had to maintain services unaided when *ME* was withdrawn, and until *Prince* was ready for service the start of the summer service had to be deferred. To assist, *Linda* was hired from the Penrhyn Quarries, who had just closed their main line. She arrived at Minffordd by rail and on Sunday 15 July, there were three engines in steam at Boston

Lodge. *Prince* had problems for several days; *Linda* had no vacuum ejector and only limited water capacity, and, with solid bronze axleboxes, was prone to run these hot. That summer was one of the worst for the burning of midnight oil, either to repair *Prince* or the *Earl,* or to remove *Linda's* wheels to clean up the hot bearings. Nevertheless, records were again broken that year, with 114,000 passenger journeys made.

1963 marked the Centenary of the introduction of steam locomotives on the Festiniog, and special celebrations and publicity were arranged which again helped to boost receipts. It also marked the introduction to service of the ex-Lynton and Barnstaple Coach as a real Buffet Car, with cooking facilities, dynamo and batteries for both electric light and fridge, and an enlarged profile. This coach was the prototype for all the new corridor coaches and immediately became extremely popular. It meant that for the two train service a Buffet Car was available for both train sets, and the four wheelers, known as the Bug Boxes, could become spare vehicles attached to the front of any train. The 3.00 pm train which normally ran non-stop became known as "Y Cymro" (The Welshman) and carried a headboard. *Linda* had been equipped with a vacuum ejector, and attached to one of the old wooden framed England tenders (built for *Prince* and his sisters) with three oil barrels and suitable piping to provide a reserve of water and coal. At first she was only used to a limited extent, mostly double heading *Prince,* but as *Linda* proved herself very useful and some of the problems got ironed out, so she was used more regularly on her own. When she had first arrived I made her my special responsibility, particularly in view of her lack of vacuum equipment and shortage of water capacity, as well as the somewhat experimental nature of some of the alterations we were making, and I kept her as my special engine for several years.

CHAPTER XII

On to Dduallt

The usefulness of *Linda* prompted negotiations for her purchase and also her twin sister *Blanche,* and a package deal was negotiated with the Penrhyn Quarry Company to acquire the two engines and also the rails and chairs of their main line, the rails being bull head of similar section to that on part of the FR, though in 24 instead of 30 foot lengths. *Blanche* arrived, by road, in December 1963, but it was early 1965 before the first consignment of rail, lifted and transported by a contractor, arrived at Minffordd.

In 1964 details were announced of the scheme devised by Gerald Fox for diverting the line past the CEGB lake at Tanygrisiau, incorporating a spiral around the hill beside Dduallt Station so as to gain height. This hill was given to the railway by one of our good friends, Mr Evershed, and that enabled work to start. The first sod was dug by Dr. Michael Lewis, then of Cambridge, on 2 January 1965, at a spot near Dduallt Station, now marked by a suitably inscribed stone. For the first few years, digging continued in a small way to create this first part of the spiral, the cuttings being dug from either end to create the adjoining embankments. Rock was very soon struck, so that drilling and blasting became necessary. This required a compressed air supply and tools, which meant money, and so started arguments between those wanting the available cash generated from the passenger receipts to be used for improving facilities to the public – particularly new coaches – which would, in its turn, create more revenue, and those wanting money for the deviation which would not bring any benefit to the organisation for what looked like an eternity. On the other hand, volunteers were slowly constructing earthworks for a new railway at minimal cost.

1965 was a special year in many ways. In March Moyra and I became engaged; we had known each other for several years through our old time dancing activities. On the FR it marked the centenary of the introduction of passenger services, for the Festiniog was a pioneer in carrying passengers on the narrow gauge. To celebrate, it had been decided to inaugurate the observation car with a suitable ceremony and number it 100, and to re-number the prototype new carriage from 24 to 104. This coach had run on temporary bogies during August 1963, to help relieve the pressure on accommodation, and had properly entered traffic in 1964. 1965 also saw *Blanche* running in proper Festiniog livery with a new tender, after a

133

Digging out a cutting for the Deviation in May 1973.

season with the same temporary tender, no. 38, that *Linda* had first used. It was also the year when work started on the track above Tanybwlch towards Ddaullt. The track up to Tanybwlch was no longer giving the same anxiety, though it was still far from being so good that there could be complacency.

The work was given a good start when I was approached by the Commanding Officer of the 16 Railway Training Regiment, R.E. the permanent unit at Longmoor, for training facilities for his men. What he wanted was to take his men to a 'strange' railway which they could take over and operate, whilst camping in the locality. This gave them experience in living away from base and under canvas, and working with a civilian railway authority. In return for the use of the line, they wanted to do work which would benefit the FR, and we suggested the relaying of the first stretch above Tanybwlch. As we had to operate advertised train services, we had our own drivers on the engines, and guards on the passenger trains to look after the tickets, etc., but there were plenty of extra trains to run, for VIP visitors as well as for taking rails, sleepers, ballast, etc., from Minffordd for the relaying operation. The weather was as wet as it could be, and the campsite, opposite Minffordd Station, became a quagmire. Mother and Father were up for part of the period and Father was invited, with me, to the dinner night at the Officer's Mess, which entailed splashing through the mud in our wellies, in evening dress!

As soon as they cleared up, the sun came out, and we then had a spell of beautiful weather, leading up to our Wedding Day.

After the family affair in the church and reception, we went by train to Tanybwlch, headed by *Prince* which was driven by Bill Hoole. We were treated to various excitements on the journey, varying from the usual detonators, to padlocked level crossing gates and locals waving flags at Penrhyn. After a stop in the woods, Bill put Moyra into the driver's seat, which left its mark on her dress!! Alan Pegler and other FR people gave a final send off from Tanybwlch, and we were able to clean up on the train journey from Blaenau to Llandudno Junction and Manchester en route for a week in Scotland. Without such a beautiful, warm, sunny day, we could never have enjoyed the festivities in the way we did.

When I first moved to Portmadoc I found digs, but these were not quite what I wanted, and in any case as soon as the busy season came the room was wanted for more lucrative lets. The landlady agreed to continue to provide me with meals, so I made accommodation for myself on the top floor of Harbour Station, converting the old boardroom into a bedroom and an office cum sitting room, with the two adjoining lavatories made into a bathroom. In the autumn I moved to May Jones just across the road for my meals, and she became one of the institutions of the F.R., providing meals, and in some cases lodgings, for many of the regular volunteers and long term temporary staff who were living in the accommodation we were creating in Harbour Station. The large room which Robert Evans had used as his office, which had drawers and cupboards full of drawings and archives, made a good place for my 0 gauge railway, for which we took in electricity, as the room only had gas, like much of the station. At quieter times, some of the others in the station would join in on operating sessions, which frequently included beer trains to keep the operators going!

My car lived in the Goods Shed; when I was first there I had an M.G. 'T.C.' but this was written off by an army lorry on the Cob one Saturday night as I was returning from working at Boston Lodge. The Cob was blocked for some time, and the army had to get heavy lifting gear from South Wales, but the rest of the gang from Boston Lodge, with the help of friends at a local garage, got the M.G. back to the garage, even if its noise going down the High Street woke up many of the locals.

Although life was fairly hectic, particularly in the summer, I was able to continue with my old time dancing, one or two evenings a week, even going seriously enough for Moyra and I to pass some medal tests. In the mid 60s the Blaenau Ffestiniog Music Society decided to put on a performance of Gilbert and Sullivan's H.M.S. Pinafore, and as this was something I had done at school and in Germany, Moyra and I joined them. This was the first time G & S had been done locally, but Barmouth followed the example with Pirates of Penzance, which we also joined, but it was a little too far to travel in the winter. Blaenau then did The Mikado and asked me to produce it, something I had never tackled before, and although I enjoyed it, it was very hard work, as we only just had enough people, with little choice for the principals. It was extremely difficult to get the necessary people together for rehearsals but nevertheless we all enjoyed doing them, and the audiences supported us well. Moyra and I found ourselves on the Music Society Committee; I did a year as chairman and then became treasurer.

After our marriage the Company made the whole of the top floor of

Allan as a sailor in the Blaenau Musical Society production of HMS Pinafore in 1965.

Harbour Station into a very nice flat for us. As things continued to grow, so we got rather fed up with being right on top of the job, and moved to Minffordd to a bungalow from where I could cycle to and from work.

Following the start made by the army in 1965 the Permanent Way people had to continue to do the major relaying work on the Portmadoc to Tanybwlch stretch during the winter but in the summer work continued on relaying above Tanybwlch. This stretch had rail in poor condition generally, so it was relaid completely with the ex Penrhyn Quarry rail, though, unfortunately, on soft wood sleepers, as this was before we had adopted Jarrah hardwood as standard.

The great traffic explosion was taking place at that time, with fantastic traffic increases each year. Fortunately the arrival of the Penrhyn engines had solved our Motive Power problems; they proved to be strong, rugged and reliable machines that were able to work the services with almost monotonous regularity. In 1966 *ME* was only available as a reserve, *Earl* was still under repairs, so *Linda* and *Blanche,* with *Prince* for the lighter trains, had to maintain the service which they did virtually without problems.

By the winter of 1967/68, everything was all set for opening to Dduallt the following Easter. The deviationists were digging out rock to make way for a run round loop at Dduallt without having to take down too many of the trees which helped to make the station so attractive, as the additional rock was needed to complete the embankment to form the first part of the spiral, but just when everything seemed to be going reasonably well, disaster struck from a distance. A foot and mouth epidemic occurred in the border counties and the local farmers were naturally most concerned lest the disease should spread into the area. Not only did we have to stop volunteers with cars, but everyone was asked to avoid travel through the infected area, and so much of our winter programme of work was seriously delayed. However, when the position eased, volunteers rallied round in the usual way, and trains did start to run from Dduallt, as planned, on 6 April. There was no grand opening, just *Earl of Merioneth* on a nine coach train, but as the deviationists had not finished their work, there was no run round loop and an engine had to be in the siding at Dduallt to bring the train down, the train engine then dropping into the siding to do the same for the next train – at the busier times – or following down to Tanybwlch to change engines at slacker times, leaving the "Dduallt pilot", probably *Prince,* to work any PW trains until the next up train.

By 20 May the loop was completed, and then services settled down as planned, but spring Bank Holiday week gave a taste of things to come, with queues for trains. People had said that the proposed peak timetable, with three train sets, crossing at Minffordd and Tanybwlch, was unworkable, but to increase capacity the timetable was abandoned on the Wednesday, with trains being turned round and run as frequently as possible, so that the 16.50 train in fact left at 16.10, the first train of the day to have spare seats, and there was another train to follow. For the next day, it was therefore decided to take advantage of the short trains being operated and use Penrhyn for passing to operate a 45 minute service, starting at 10.30 am and finishing with a 17.15 pm. Everything went splendidly, minimising queueing and showing what could be achieved. Due to the foot and mouth epidemic, some of the coaches expected for service in the summer were not completed, so it was decided that Penrhyn should be used as well as Minffordd, and a 45 minute service was operated, Monday to Thursday, during the afternoon, but the Controller, that person who sits in an office at Portmadoc supervising the working of the trains, would sometimes arrange for them to cross at Minffordd if one was running late, and it would thus reduce delays.

With the trains running the extra distance to Dduallt, if only a similar number of passengers had travelled, the higher fares would have yielded welcome additional income, but in fact the traffic numbers increased by 33 per cent to 294,000 journeys, and traffic receipts were up by 60 per cent. However, the additional distance was showing in the mileages worked by engines and carriages – *Blanche* 5,823, *Earl* 5,697, *Linda* 4,330, *Prince* 3,806 or 24,427 locomotive miles compared with 19,033 in 1967. Some of the modern carriages ran over 16,000 miles and the total carriage miles were 123,002 as against 78,441 in 1967. *Blanche's* and *Linda's* mileages may not look very high in terms of motor cars, or even standard gauge engines, but if you think of their 2 ft. diameter wheels as against a main line mixed traffic engine with over 6 ft. wheels and multiply the mileage by three, it looks a little different, since it is revolutions which really count. Also it must not be overlooked that engines on the FR tend to be flogged unmercifully to the maximum the boilers can produce, and if a Black 5 hauled a load of five or six times its own weight up a 1 in 70 gradient, and did it regularly, enthusiasts would have been flocking to see it. Not only that, but *Linda* and *Blanche* hauled such loads at 15 to 20 mph, which in terms of wheel revolutions corresponds to 50 or so mph of their big brethren.

The success of the season did enable the company to order two new Fairlie boilers, with superheaters, from Hunslet Engine Company of Leeds, who were able to offer advantageous terms, as they had not a lot of work in their boiler shop. This was in addition to the fitting of *Linda's* boiler with a new steel firebox and superheater that winter which had already been planned.

The next decade saw continued development on the ten miles between Portmadoc and Dduallt, with more new carriages, track continually improving with fresh flat bottom rail obtained secondhand, and all major resleepering done with new Jarrah hardwood sleepers, laid on new stone ballast. This gave a permanent way second to none, and greatly improved the comfort of the passengers, as well as enabling a steady increase in speeds. Traffic continued to increase to a peak in 1974, when 235,000 people made 418,000 journeys.

The deviationists were able to start work on the west side of the lake at Dduallt in 1968, and the whole of the spiral took shape with the bridge at the south end of the station taking the new line over the old. Discussions with the CEGB at last resolved the problem of the second portion of the route to Tanygrisiau and the west side route, going behind the Power Station, was agreed. The final Lands Tribunal heard the FRs further case for compensation, and awarded a substantial sum (£65,000 with interest

Father and Mother in the garden at Cheam

to bring it to over £100,000) a legal case which had dragged on for a record 16 years.

The locomotives underwent a very significant change; oil was introduced as the fuel to make the steam instead of coal. The Forestry people, who had been planting more and more areas either side of the railway, were getting increasingly concerned about the damage done by lineside fires, which sometimes spread up the hillsides, and the company's insurers were objecting to the claims they were having to meet. *Linda* was the first to be converted to burn oil, and after some trials and tribulations, it was made to work so successfully that the load haulage capacity was considerably increased, and the fuel costs considerably reduced. It also made the superheating really work, and in 1971 when a superheated *Linda* was running alongside a saturated *Blanche, Linda* was using about 20% less oil than *Blanche*, and at the same time was capable of hauling very much heavier loads. *Blanche* was then fitted with a superheater also, and as the new Fairlie boilers had been provided with them, today they are standard on all FR engines.

1972 was a year marked by sadness for both myself and the FR. Father died in his sleep early on 9 August. Though we knew that it could happen, it was not particularly expected. On the FR, Alan Pegler had to resign as Chairman of the company, owing to his unfortunate financial disaster through taking *Flying Scotsman* to America. He had wanted me to go to the States for a short period to help him with the engine; Bill Harvey had done so, but whilst I would dearly have loved to have had the opportunity, I felt that my first duties lay at Portmadoc, and the railway hadn't quite got organised enough for it to be left, particularly in the operating season. AFP, as he is usually known, was a real gentleman for whom I shall always have great respect. Once he thought it would be better if I would leave the FR, and he summoned Father to London to tell him, but subsequently he realised that there was another side to the story. Not only did he give me all the support I needed, but he wrote, in his own fair hand, and apologised for what had happened. We can all make mistakes, but it takes a gentleman to apologise. He always had time to speak to anyone and everyone, and was friendly to all the staff and volunteers alike, an attribute essential in an organisation such as the FR, which relies on dedicated workers, paid and voluntary, for its success.

THE FESTINIOG RAILWAY
is ALIVE
– help
it to
grow

Details from
R H R Garraway 35 Holmwood Road Cheam Surrey

CHAPTER XIII

Blaenau Ffestiniog

With the injection of capital from the CEGB compensation, funds became available for some developments which would hopefully produce additional revenue to help finance the completion of restoration to Blaenau. The 1969 Development of Tourism Act enabled the Wales Tourist Board to give grants to assist projects, and the FR company immediately sought assistance from this source for everything possible.

A new crossing loop at Rhiw Goch, new carriages, a new link building at Harbour Station all got help from the WTB, as well as other projects to extend the railway back to Blaenau. The new loop was needed because as traffic had grown, the additional coaches had made it impossible to continue to use Penrhyn, which could not be enlarged any more due to lack of space.

With the completion of the first section of the Deviation, it was desirable to use it to earn more revenue, and in 1975 a shuttle service was operated with a diesel and one coach on a push pull basis from Dduallt to Gelliwiog. Due to the problems of crowds on the main trains, passengers were reluctant to leave their seats at Dduallt to go on the extra ride, for fear that they would not get on another train to get back, and only some 1,400 people actually made the additional journey. This proved a point which many of us had stoutly maintained in 1967/68. A number of people had suggested then that a separate service should operate from Tanybwlch to Dduallt, the main trains only running between Portmadoc and Tanybwlch. However, I had argued that people would not change trains. The argument still arises from time to time.

Construction of the new 300 yard tunnel started that year, and with it in progress the shuttle could not run in 1976. A condition of the grant given by the WTB for the tunnel was that it should be brought into use as soon as it was completed, so it was decided to put in a temporary terminus beside the Tanygrisiau lake, called Llyn Ystradau, and run services to there for the 1977 season. Unfortunately, the rock through which the tunnel had been bored proved to be not so solid as expected as it was only very few feet below the surface; there had been much debate as to whether it should be a tunnel or cutting and I was one who wanted the latter. It was necessary to line the tunnel in several places, and it was decided to do this by a shotcreting process, which consisted of spraying concrete onto the walls with a suitable hardening agent to make the con-

Linda *and train passing the new loop at Rhiw Goch with partially completed 110 in the siding, in May 1976.*

crete set quickly. This operation was beset with many problems, not helped by the fact that the Readymix Concrete had to travel by road from Minffordd to railhead by Llyn Ystradau Station, and then be transferred into a special rail wagon for transport to the plant in the tunnel actually doing the spraying. After it was done, there were places where too much had gone on, making the tunnel too small, so that it was the beginning of July before the consulting engineers and Railway Inspectorate were satisfied and would allow trains to commence running to Llyn Ystradau. The official opening ceremonies actually took place a fortnight earlier, having been arranged long in advance, and this produced publicity so that passengers came expecting to travel over the new stretch and were very disappointed when they found they could not do so.

When the decision had been taken to put in a temporary terminus at Llyn Ystradau, no one could see exactly how it would be possible to build the last portion of new line behind the Power Station, because the CEGB insisted that the work be done by an approved contractor in a period of nine months. With the inflation of the mid 70s, our finances from the compensation and other sources just could not meet this task, but then the

Government announced its Manpower Service Commission Schemes which paid for the employment of people, on tasks which otherwise would not be done by charitable organisations. The FR Trust, being a charity, was eligible for such a scheme, and a package deal was negotiated with Sir Robert McAlpine, contractors approved by the CEGB, to manage the contract, and work started. The volunteer deviationists continued with some tasks, particularly the bridge over the Cwmorthin River by Tanygrisiau Station, using precast concrete beams.

There were the usual struggles to complete the essentials for opening to Tanygrisiau, but the opening took place, on a very wet day, 24 June, by Dewi Rees of the MSC. From being a railway offering a ride from Portmadoc up into the hills, it became one readily accessible at both ends. The FR was back in Blaenau Ffestiniog, as Tanygrisiau is a suburb of

Merddin Emrys *and* Earl of Merioneth *double heading a special at Porthmadog on 4th May 1980.*

Blaenau, and is only a mile from the BR station. A local bus service was introduced connecting FR to BR, giving a dramatic increase in the through traffic from BR. After a couple of years in which the numbers of passenger journeys had dropped below 400,000, 1978 gave 410,000, and it was hoped that with the connection to North Wales, things would improve again.

In 1976 the local Councils had approached us regarding the site for our terminus in Blaenau. We had been looking at various options, and had negotiated that a tip clearance scheme being done should grade an area opposite the BR station in such a way as to be suitable for our terminus. The local councils were concerned that this site was too far away from the centre of the town, and that when we ran to it, there would consequently only be minimal benefit to the shops, etc. We had always said that we would be quite prepared to go further into Blaenau, but that someone else would have to foot the bill since it would bring no financial benefit to the FR, and on the contrary, would give us an extra quarter mile of track to operate and maintain, besides not providing such an attractively situated station. When we had a meeting on site we first looked at the old Duffws terminus, but the site was not long enough for today's trains, and would involve a crossing of BR lines, as well as having other problems. The best which could be suggested was the site of the old GW station – "Central" – where we had long felt our terminus should be.

As the meeting was ending the thought struck me that since BR tracks were already there, why could not their station be there as well. We didn't want to have two FR stations close together, so the Council Officials went away to get consulting engineers to look at the practicalities of the scheme, and talk with BR. Funding was negotiated from various sources, and a total scheme was devised to improve roads, provide car parking space, form bus stands and open up the centre of the town. Unfortunately, the funds available did not run to all it had hoped to do, and various things had either to be cut out or cheapened.

Building the FRs new Moelwyn Tunnel had cost a lot more than budgeted for, likewise with completing the Deviation to Tanygrisiau, so that the company had had to borrow far too heavily from its Bank. This had all produced very many internal problems within the organisation, problems which bedevil many organisations run by a mix of volunteers and professionals, and as a result a retired senior officer from ICI, P.R. Wollan, was brought in as Chief Executive.

There was pressure from the Councils for us to complete restoration of the Tanygrisiau – Blaenau stretch and start running to the new terminus as soon as it was finished, but the FR was also under pressure from the CEGB to finish off a number of things, particularly of a landscaping nature, between the tunnel and Tanygrisiau, and we had wanted to digest and consolidate before undertaking work towards Blaenau. As soon as he arrived, Dick Wollan said that it was essential that going through to Blaenau was done without incurring any cost to company funds, and by skilful negotiation with various authorities, he was able to achieve this. In

144

The start of work by FR volunteers at Blaenau new station.

March 1983 BR moved into their new station, and on May 23rd I drove a training train through to Blaenau with *Linda*, 150 years to the day since the original Act forming the Company had been signed. Two days later great celebrations were held for the resumption of train services over the whole length of the FR. We had accomplished what we had set out to do some 31 years previously. As mentioned earlier a small group of the original people who had started it all going, got together for an informal celebration; it was a great shame that one absentee on that day was Alan Pegler, who, on the same day, was involved with the launching of the revived Venice Simplon Orient Express.

Although 1982 and the opening to Blaenau gave a small boost to the

The new station at Blaenau, with the SLOA Pullman special train and Earl of Merioneth.

Festiniog traffic results, they still remained very disappointing. What was particularly interesting was that traffic coming in off BR doubled compared with the previous year, and became somewhere about 20 per cent of the business. It was also noticeable that although the numbers of journeys slightly declined in 1983, the number of people, or tickets issued, remained similar, because of all the through tour bookings.

CHAPTER XIV

All change for Scotland

Looking back over my life I have been fortunate in that on several occasions circumstances have just been right for me to seize a new opportunity.

It was the War and the evacuation of The Leys School which took me to Scotland. I clearly remember the journey North in 1940 with the thrill of seeing Scotland for the first time and my frustration when it got dark. The next day we could see the glorious view to Ben Vrackie from the Atholl Palace Hotel, which we all climbed as soon as possible. With my enthusiasm for cycling I saw much of the area, including one tour north over Drumochter, west to Fort William (arriving in a thunderstorm), south over Rannoch Moor in glorious sunshine, and back past Loch Tay to find most expeditions that week-end had been abandoned due to bad weather. A quartet of us, using railwaymen's cheap travel, did a tour which introduced me to some of the finest railway journeys of the country. It seemed like a disaster when I was called up into the army, but I got in just before National Service started, trained at Longmoor and arrived at the Detmold Military Railway for its last months of British Military operation.

Leslie Parker appointed me to the new job with responsibility for A.T.C. just as it was at its most interesting stage of development, and with steam at some of its finest hours, yet as dieselisation loomed the Festiniog opening arose.

In the early 1950's the Festiniog Railway took most of my time until I introduced Moyra to the beauties of Scotland with a tour by train. Our honeymoon was another tour by train, and since then we have toured Scotland nearly every year, with Mother and Auntie as well for some years. Moyra and I had talked about retiring to Scotland, but then another Railway started to claim my attention.

When we were trying to make *Linda* work satisfactorily on oil firing, John Patterson of Laidlaw Drew in Edinburgh, who had supplied the equipment, sent me a copy of a reply to Mr. E.V. Cooper regarding converting small standard gauge engines to oil firing. I then discovered that it was the Eric Cooper who, when living at Derby, had put the first Gardner diesel engine into *Moelwyn*, and that he was chairman of a scheme attempting to restore train services on a section of the old Highland Railway main line, recently closed by B.R. between Aviemore and Grantown-on-Spey.

In Chapter XIII I made reference to internal problems within the FR organisation. For various reasons the permanent staff revived the association with the NUR for staff representation and negotiation, which had existed in pre-war days. This brought fresh problems both for myself and the Board, of which few of us had much experience. In 1977 Bill Broadbent, Festiniog Society Chairman and Company Director, was not fully occupied and came to Porthmadog as Chief Executive. He left at the end of the year without having enough time to make a permanent contribution to the management and industrial relations problems.

The Board had decided to reorganise the management structure of the Company by having a full time Chief Executive with primary responsibilities and for me to have a subsidiary task of looking after operational and engineering matters only. I was by no means keen on this scheme, and went through a very difficult period indeed, but fortunately Dick Hardy, with his considerable experience of railways and staff negotiations, had just joined the Board. Taken somewhat aback at what was happening, he was able to pour oil onto the troubled waters and help resolve the problems. Consultants were brought in, and soon after the reopening to Tanygrisiau they visited the railway and had discussions with both myself and the other managers. Their verdict was that someone *was* needed to steer the railway who had been an experienced business executive in one of the large organisations, who had retired early and was interested in a relatively small but challenging task to which a great deal could be given. Not knowing what was going to happen to me, I had been looking at one or two alternatives and had applied for other jobs. I was fortunate in being accepted for one with the Railway Inspectorate, which I would have liked very much if it had not meant living near London, but it relieved my immediate anxieties at the crucial time, though I finally turned it down as matters became resolved.

The Consultants were as good as their word, and found exactly the man in P.R. (Dick) Wollan, who was retiring from ICI. The Directors gave me encouraging reports, and when I met him for the first time at a Board Meeting in January 1979 I immediately took to him. He visited the railway with his wife and Moyra and I went up with them to Tanygrisiau and immediately felt we had found some real new friends. He started work (officially only part time) after Easter, and although it meant that I was no longer 'King of the Castle', I was still G.M. He ensured that I still remained an important element in the hierarchy, and I look back on the years working with Dick with pleasure; never once did I feel that I had a boss sitting across the corridor who was watching everything I was doing but I felt I had a friend to work with, who I could consult on any difficulty or problem. When Dick first arrived he told me that we were not going to duplicate work and activities; he would take over some matters and deal with them completely, but similarly he would leave me alone to deal with matters I was looking after. Nevertheless we each usually managed to keep each other up to date in matters we were dealing with, and the progress of our activities. He was a chemist by training, and had a very keen and clever mind. Early in his career he had specialised in Management, which he believed to be an art and skill in its own right, for which appropriate training was essential. It should not be regarded as just another step in the ladder, but should have its own line of promotion separate from commercial, engineering or financial ladders. I learnt quite a lot from him – more if I could remember it – and I value the experience of working with him. In the 4½ years we worked together we never had a cross word, nor did I ever rebel against any decision he made, even if I did not wholly agree with it, and we remain good friends.

For some time two FR stalwarts had been striving to obtain some form of official recognition for my efforts on the FR. I felt that that was not the sort of thing for which awards were given, but when a letter from the Prime Minister's office arrived in the post, Moyra was agog for me to come home and open it, and it was a great surprise to read that they wanted to know whether I would accept an award if it was offered. It was a particularly great honour to me, as it was the first time any award had been made to anyone in the independent railway movement, and the pleasure of going to Buckingham Palace to receive the MBE from the Queen herself, actually on our wedding anniversary, was something we shall never forget.

It was a beautiful day, and as we came out of the Palace, waiting at the gates was Alan Pegler himself, who walked with us across Green Park. On the day that the awards had been published he had been up early scanning the papers and telling everyone, and in the evening after the presentation the Board had arranged a party at the Banquet of the Beefeater by the Tower, at which at that time Alan P. was Master of Ceremonies. He told the whole Banquet not only where we had been that morning, but that it was our wedding anniversary, and he had had a special gateau made for us and our party. All very typical of AFP who had a marvellous gentlemanly way of enhancing great occasions.

Dick Wollan soon found that what he had intended as a part time job was very much full time, particularly with the task of the final completion to Blaenau Ffestiniog. His work took a lot of the load off my shoulders which meant that, though I was still working more or less 7 days a week, I could get away more easily, particularly in the summer months. Eric Cooper approached me as to whether I could help with some problems with the class 5, no. 5025, at Aviemore which had some valve peculiarities. As we could not finish it on the first visit, Eric offered me the use of a spare compartment in their sleeping coach, which led me to make more visits.

We had been following progress towards reopening to Boat of Garten, and had met Eric on site each year when we had been on holiday. Although I found standard gauge engine parts heavy after years on the narrow gauge, I found that it had its own appeal once again. In 1981 and 1982 we took a cottage in Boat of Garten for working holidays on the railway, and when some bungalows were being built overlooking the station we decided to buy one so that we could spend even more holidays and long week ends there together, Moyra having come under the spell of Boat of Garten as much as I.

I had always intimated that I wanted to retire at 60 if possible, and once the Festiniog had got established through to Blaenau, Dick Wollan indicated that he did not want to carry on any longer at the tempo at which he had been working. We agreed that management of the type of business that the FR had become was not what I wanted. Dick was able to negotiate satisfactory terms for me to continue on a consultancy basis until I could start drawing my pension, which he had likewise organised. The FR found a new GM in David Pollock, an ex-managing director of the Westinghouse Brake & Signal Coy, who took over in August 1983.

In my last months I had been involved, on a consultancy basis, with the planning of the railway for the International Garden Festival at Liverpool held in 1984. Various options had been considered, including trams, but 15" gauge was selected, largely because the Romney Hythe and Dymchurch Railway had surplus engines and some carriages which it was prepared to hire to the Festival. There were increasing problems in fitting in the railway to the architects requirements, and gradients and curves got more severe and sharper, and in retrospect I feel a 2' gauge line might have been more suitable, if sufficiently powerful locomotives could have been found and made available. Fortunately they did, in the end, accept my recommendation for a manager, and when the Romney engines supplied did not come up to haulage expectations, he was able to negotiate with the Ravenglass and Eskdale Railway for the hire of one of theirs.

With our own cottage at Boat of Garten we spent longer week ends there in 1983 as well as all holidays. It had been intended that I should join the Strathspey Board but for various reasons this did not take place until Eric Cooper had an unfortunate disagreement with his fellow Directors, and I was co-opted in his place. I was sorry about this as I had been looking forward to joining Eric and working with him again.

Dick Wollan and I had expected to hand over slowly to David Pollock, but Dick finished completely at the end of September, and I soon found that what little part time work I was doing could easily be done from anywhere, particularly when our typist left and I started having to type my own letters. It was agreed that I need have no obligation to attend the office regularly and so we accelerated plans to build a bungalow for ourselves at Boat of Garten, and move there permanently. We now have a home on what was once part of the Great North of Scotland locomotive depot, later an outpost of the LNER.

I left BR when the end of steam was announced, and the only railways on which steam looked likely to continue were the narrow gauge ones. For 25 years and more the Festiniog was my whole life, but bit by bit its attractions to me have diminished, and many of my dreams and aspirations have been lost. Now the wheel has turned full circle, and I am back with standard gauge steam, in circumstances reminiscent of the happy years with the Festiniog. I still have my contacts with other small railways through my chairmanship of the Association of Minor Railways, an organisation going back to before the War, which I was instrumental in

AVIEMORE SPEYSIDE station is situated just beyond the BR station and is linked to the town by a pedestrian underpass. Just beyond lies the railways AVIEMORE WORKS, housed in a stone built shed of 1897. Here locomotives and rolling stock are maintained and repaired.

All trackwork in the works yard was relaid by volunteer labour.

Gentle gradients carry the line over the SUMMIT and down through woodlands into BOAT OF GARTEN, named after a ferry of a previous age and once the junction for the GREAT NORTH of SCOTLAND RAILWAY.

The track bed to GRANTOWN on SPEY is also owned by Strathspey Railway.

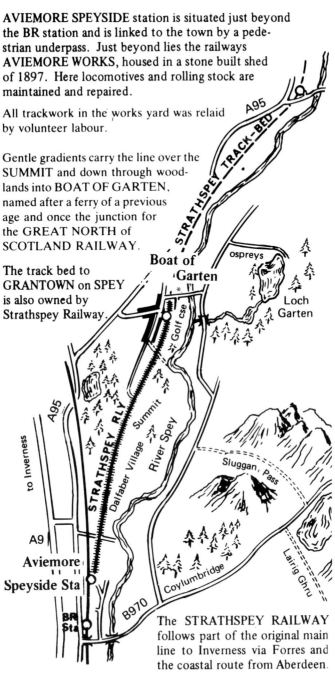

The STRATHSPEY RAILWAY follows part of the original main line to Inverness via Forres and the coastal route from Aberdeen.

Built in 1863 by the Perth and Inverness Junction Railway [later to become part of the Highland Railway] it was relegated to secondary status on completion of the more direct line from Aviemore via Carr Bridge.

Location of our bungalow, on the site of the GNSR Loco Shed Yard.

The author back with the standard gauge at Aviemore on his appointment to the Board of the Strathspey Railway Co.

reviving to provide a forum for the management of the operating railways. We work very closely with the Association of Railway Preservation Societies, for whom I am Operating Adviser.

Now I look forward to spending my years of retirement trying to help

152

Britain's most northerly voluntarily run railway, which I am hoping will become an even greater attraction in what I regard as one of the most beautiful parts of the country. I am hoping that this may be as rewarding and exciting as those early years of the Festiniog, and perhaps in years to come it will itself make more chapters to this story.

INDEX

FESTINIOG RAILWAY COMPANY

TIME TABLE - 1959

WEEKDAYS ONLY, 16th MAY–26th SEPTEMBER, also 28th and 30th MARCH

SUNDAYS, 29th MARCH, 17th MAY and Sundays during AUGUST

WEDNESDAYS ONLY,

1st APRIL–13th MAY and 30th SEPTEMBER to 14th OCTOBER

(See Note A)

	Pwllheli	dep.	9S45	9E55	12.45	4.5	
	Portmadoc (W)	arr.	10S18	10E23	1.14		
	Minffordd	arr.				4.42	
	Barmouth	dep.		9.25	12.25	3E45	
	Minffordd	arr.		10.12	1.12	4E31	
	Portmadoc (W)	arr.		10.16	1.16		

			B				C
0	Portmadoc (Harbour)	dep.	10.40	2.30		4.30	7.30
¾	Pen Cob (Halt)	,,	dd	dd		dd	......
1	Boston Lodge (Halt)	,,	dd	dd		dd	dd
2	Minffordd (for B.R. (W))	,,	10.52	2.42		4.44	dd
2¾	Pen-y-Bryn (Halt)	,,	dd	dd		dd	......
3¼	Penrhyn	,,	10.58	2.48		4.50	dd
7½	Tan-y-Bwlch	arr.	11.25	3.15		5.15	8.10
9	Dduallt	⎫					
12	Tan-y-Grisiau	⎬ Service temporarily suspended					
13¼	Blaenau Ffestiniog	⎭					

0	Blaenau Ffestiniog	⎫					
1¼	Tan-y-Grisiau	⎬ Service temporarily suspended					
4¼	Dduallt	⎭	B				C
5¾	Tan-y-Bwlch	dep.	11.45	3.30		5.30	8.40
10	Penrhyn	,,	12.12	3.57		5.57	dd
10½	Pen-y-Bryn (Halt)	,,	dd	dd		dd	......
11¼	Minffordd (for B.R. (W))	,,	12.18	4.03		6.03	dd
12¼	Boston Lodge (Halt)	,,	dd	dd		dd	dd
12½	Pen Cob (Halt)	,,	dd	dd		dd	......
13¼	Portmadoc (Harbour)	arr.	12.30	4.15		6.15	9.20

Portmadoc (W)	dep.	1.17	4.38			
Minffordd	dep.	1.22	4.42		6.11	
Barmouth	arr.	2.12	5.27		7.2	
Minffordd	dep.		4E31		6E25	
Portmadoc (W)	dep.	1.20	4E40	4S35	6E33	6S27
Pwllheli	arr.	1.55	5E20	5S5	7E2	7S00

Western Region times shown apply 15th June–12th September, week-days only.

A. On Wednesdays only, 1st April–13th May and 30th September–14th October, also Sundays during August and Sundays 29th March and 17th May the 3.30 train will leave Tan-y-Bwlch at 3.45 and run 15 minutes later throughout. The 4.30 from Portmadoc and 5.30 from Tan-y-Bwlch will not run.

B. Runs 6th July–12th September, week-days only, also Whit Monday, 18th May.

C. Runs Tuesday, Wednesday and Thursday only, 14th July–27th August, also Saturday and Whit Monday, May 26th and 28th and Saturday and Monday, August 1st and 3rd.

Trains marked B and C may also run on other days by prior arrangement.

E. Except Saturdays.   S. Saturdays only.

dd Calls when required to set down on notice to the Guard at previous stopping station; passengers wishing to join should give the necessary hand signal to the Driver.

T. STEPHENSON & SONS LTD., PRINTERS, PRESCOT, LANCS.

Books from Middleton Press

BRANCH LINES
Vic Mitchell and Keith Smith

BRANCH LINES TO MIDHURST	0 906520 01 0
BRANCH LINES TO HORSHAM	0 906520 02 9
BRANCH LINE TO SELSEY	0 906520 04 5
BRANCH LINES TO EAST GRINSTEAD	0 906520 07 X
BRANCH LINES TO ALTON	0 906520 11 8
BRANCH LINE TO HAYLING	0 906520 12 6
BRANCH LINE TO SOUTHWOLD	0 906520 15 0
BRANCH LINE TO TENTERDEN	0 906520 21 5

SOUTH COAST RAILWAYS
Vic Mitchell and Keith Smith

BRIGHTON TO WORTHING	0 906520 03 7
WORTHING TO CHICHESTER	0 906520 06 1
CHICHESTER TO PORTSMOUTH	0 906520 14 2
BRIGHTON TO EASTBOURNE	0 906520 16 9
RYDE TO VENTNOR	0 906520 19 3

STEAMING THROUGH
Peter Hay

STEAMING THROUGH KENT	0 906520 13 4
STEAMING THROUGH EAST HANTS	0 906520 18 5
STEAMING THROUGH EAST SUSSEX	0 906520 22 3

OTHER RAILWAY BOOKS

INDUSTRIAL RAILWAYS OF THE SOUTH-EAST	0 906520 09 6
WAR ON THE LINE The official history of the SR in World War II	0 906520 10 X

OTHER SUSSEX BOOKS

MIDHURST TOWN – THEN & NOW	0 906520 05 3
EAST GRINSTEAD – THEN & NOW	0 906520 17 7
THE GREEN ROOF OF SUSSEX A refreshing amble along the South Downs Way.	0 906520 08 8